MESSY MORALITY

Tony Coady explores the challenges that morality poses to politics. He confronts the complex intellectual tradition known as realism, which seems to deny any relevance of morality to politics, especially international politics. He argues that, although realism has many serious faults, it has lessons to teach us: in particular, it cautions us against the dangers of moralism in thinking about politics and particularly foreign affairs. Morality must not be confused with moralism: Coady characterizes various forms of moralism and sketches their distorting influence on a realistic political morality. He seeks to restore the concept of ideals to an important place in philosophical discussion, and to give it a particular pertinence in the discussion of politics. He deals with the fashionable idea of 'dirty hands', according to which good politics will necessarily involve some degree of moral taint or corruption. Finally, he examines the controversial issue of the role of lying and deception in politics. Along the way Coady offers illuminating discussion of historical and current political controversies. This lucid book will provoke and stimulate anyone interested in the interface of morality and politics.

C. A. J. Coady was formerly Boyce Gibson Professor of Philosophy at the University of Melbourne and is now Professorial Fellow in Applied Philosophy and a Vice Chancellor's Fellow at that university. He founded and became director of the Centre for Philosophy and Public Issues, the first centre in Australia to be concerned with broad issues of philosophy and public affairs. This was absorbed into the Centre for Applied Philosophy and Public Ethics (CAPPE) of which he was deputy director for some years. His research areas include political violence, terrorism, and just war theory.

UEHIRO SERIES IN PRACTICAL ETHICS

General Editor: Julian Savulescu, University of Oxford

Choosing Children
The Ethical Dilemmas of Genetic Intervention
Jonathan Glover

Messy Morality
The Challenge of Politics
C. A. J. Coady

Messy Morality

The Challenge of Politics

C. A. J. COADY

CLARENDON PRESS · OXFORD

OXFORD
UNIVERSITY PRESS

Great Clarendon Street, Oxford OX2 6DP

Oxford University Press is a department of the University of Oxford.
It furthers the University's objective of excellence in research, scholarship,
and education by publishing worldwide in

Oxford New York

Auckland Cape Town Dar es Salaam Hong Kong Karachi
Kuala Lumpur Madrid Melbourne Mexico City Nairobi
New Delhi Shanghai Taipei Toronto

With offices in

Argentina Austria Brazil Chile Czech Republic France Greece
Guatemala Hungary Italy Japan Poland Portugal Singapore
South Korea Switzerland Thailand Turkey Ukraine Vietnam

Oxford is a registered trade mark of Oxford University Press
in the UK and in certain other countries

Published in the United States
by Oxford University Press Inc., New York

© C. A. J. Coady 2008

British Library Cataloguing in Publication Data

Data available

Library of Congress Cataloging in Publication Data

Data available

Typeset by Laserwords Private Limited, Chennai, India
Printed in Great Britain
on acid-free paper by
MPG Biddles Ltd., King's Lynn, Norfolk

ISBN 978–0–19–921208–8 (hbk); 978–0–19–959498–6 (pbk)

10 9 8 7 6 5 4 3 2 1

The Uehiro Series in Practical Ethics

In 2002 the Uehiro Foundation on Ethics and Education, chaired by Mr Eiji Uehiro, established the Uehiro Chair in Practical Ethics at the University of Oxford. The following year the Oxford Uehiro Centre for Practical Ethics was created within the Philosophy Faculty. Generous support by the Uehiro Foundation enabled the establishment of an annual lecture series, The Uehiro Lectures in Practical Ethics. These three lectures, given each year in Oxford, capture the ethos of the Oxford Uehiro Centre for Practical Ethics: to bring the best scholarship in analytic philosophy to bear on the most significant problems of our time. The aim is to make progress in the analysis and resolution of these issues to the highest academic standard in a manner that is accessible to the general public. Philosophy should not only create knowledge, it should make people's lives better. Books based upon the lectures are published by Oxford University Press in the Uehiro Series in Practical Ethics.

Julian Savulescu
Uehiro Chair in Practical Ethics
Director, Oxford Uehiro Centre for Practical Ethics
University of Oxford

Editor
The Uehiro Series in Practical Ethics

For my sons Benjamin and David and their partners Anna and Diana

Preface

This book is an expanded and modified version of the Uehiro Lectures that I gave in Oxford in May 2005. The Uehiro Lectures in Practical Ethics, an annual series of three lectures, is hosted by the Oxford Uehiro Centre for Practical Ethics. I would like to thank the benefactor of the Centre, the Uehiro Foundation on Ethics and Education of Japan, for its generous support of these lectures. I am especially grateful to the Chairman of the Foundation, Mr Eiji Uehiro, for his support. I would also like to thank the Centre's Director, Professor Julian Savulescu, for inviting me to give the lectures and for facilitating my presentation of them.

I entitled the lectures 'Messy Morality' and I've kept to that title for the book, adding the subtitle 'the Challenge of Politics' to indicate some of its primary concerns. The book expands and revises the lectures so that where there were three lectures, there are now five chapters. The first lecture has grown into two chapters and there is a final chapter on lying in politics, a topic that was only touched upon in the lectures. The themes of the book are principally concerned with the intersections of morality and politics, though it has at times a broader sweep and wider implications. I begin with a Preamble that offers a range of examples from current or past political crises that involve some of the questions posed and problems addressed in the chapters that follow. In Chapter 1 and 2, I confront the complex intellectual tradition that seems to deny any relevance of morality to politics, especially international politics. This is the tradition known as realism. I argue that, although realism has many serious faults, it has lessons to teach us that its own formulations often obscure, and that its many philosophical critics are in danger of missing. Its principal lesson, I claim, is to caution us against the dangers of moralism in thinking about politics and particularly foreign affairs. By confusing morality with moralism, and by persistently substituting a vague concept of national interest for a more robust and realistic understanding of morality, the realists blunt the importance of what they do have to teach. In these chapters, I characterize a variety of forms of moralism and sketch their distorting influence on a realistic political morality. The discussion draws upon my previously published work on moralism and realism, but gives it more focus and elaboration.

My third chapter seeks to restore the concept of ideals to an important place in philosophical discussion, and to give it a particular pertinence in the discussion of politics. When it has not been ignored or treated as an afterthought, the topic of ideals has often drawn sceptical or hostile fire from academic critics and political practitioners. Isaiah Berlin was one influential critic who argued the dangers of pursuing 'the ideal', and many of the realists treated in Chapters 1 and 2 focused some of their animus against morality in politics upon the confusing or dangerous impact of ideals. I argue that, properly understood, ideals should have an integral role in the moral life and have an important part to play in political morality. Along the way, I try to gain more conceptual clarity about ideals and their place in our moral landscape.

In the fourth chapter, I deal with the idea that good politics will necessarily involve some degree of moral taint or corruption. The idea is encapsulated in the currently fashionable concept of 'dirty hands'. This has been an important tool of philosophical analysis, especially of issues in political morality, since Michael Walzer's ground-breaking article, 'Political Action: the Problem of Dirty Hands', was published in 1973. The idea is closely related, if not identical, to that of 'supreme emergency' to which Walzer gave currency with his discussion of the Allied city bombings of World War II in his book *Just and Unjust Wars*. The concept of dirty hands is often deployed both formally amongst philosophers and more informally by practitioners of politics and policy, but it is subject to many ambiguities and difficulties of interpretation. In this chapter, I explore the meaning of the term and what validity it might have, contrasting dirty hands both with realism and with moral dilemmas, and exploring the concept and ramifications of moral corruption.

In the final chapter I address a specific form of wrongdoing that is often associated with politics, namely, lying. Although lies reside in the shadows of moral disapprobation in virtually all cultures, attitudes towards lying can be very complex and hardly anyone can seriously maintain that they have never lied. So it is not surprising to find that common attitudes towards the morality of lying run the gamut from rigorist condemnation of all lies to laxist permissiveness towards many forms of lying. Contemporary politicians are quite widely viewed as particularly prone to lying, and are often condemned for it, though they strenuously deny the specific allegations brought against them. Nor do their sins always count heavily against them with the disapproving public. This chapter explores the nature of lying and other deceptive practices with a particular eye to the philosophical tradition that includes rigorists like St Augustine and Kant, advocates of 'the noble lie' like Plato, and the relaxed, if often contorted, practitioners of casuistry.

In addition to the thanks given earlier, I would like to thank the Australian Research Council's Special Research Centre for Applied Philosophy and Public Ethics for its support of this research, and also the earlier support of the ARC for my work on 'messy morality'. My thanks also to Corpus Christi College, Oxford where I was a Visiting Fellow in the period when I delivered the lectures, and to Ned Dobos who was not only an invaluable research assistant, but helped with the editing of the book and also compiled the index. My thanks also to the publishers of the *Journal of Applied Philosophy* for permission to use some material from my paper 'The Moral Reality in Realism' which appeared in the vol. 22, no. 2, 2005 issue and which forms a basis for the much more developed treatment of issues to do with realism and moralism in Chapters 1 and 2. Finally, I profited from some helpful comments by an anonymous Oxford University Press reviewer.

Contents

Utopia and reality are thus the two facets of political science. Sound political thought and sound political life will be found where both have their place.

E. H. Carr, *The Twenty Year Crisis 1919–1939: An Introduction to the Study of International Relations*

Preamble

It may be helpful to set the scene for the detailed discussion that follows by presenting some examples of major political decisions that appear to have a moral dimension but for which problems have acutely arisen about the relevance of that dimension or the practicality of considering it.

First, there is the 2003 invasion of Iraq by a coalition led (and dominated) by the United States. The most salient public justifications for this were indeed couched in terms that have a moral overtone. Iraq was said to have had weapons of mass destruction that might be used aggressively against its neighbours and the invasion was necessary to prevent this. When Iraq turned out to have no such weapons, other reasons were brought to the fore. Iraq was supporting terrorism against the United States and others, so that the war against terror licensed the invasion. Iraq's regime was a bad one, led by the evil Saddam, and invasion was required to change it to a democracy. This in turn was demanded by humanitarian sympathy for Iraqis and by a concern for stability in the Middle East. Oil supplies to the United States and the United Kingdom needed to be secured against the malice of Saddam Hussein. Of these purported justifications, all have some moral flavouring, but the oil argument is more significantly self-interested as is the argument (seldom overtly expressed, but influential) that the massive military power of the United States should be used in favourable circumstances to assert its political domination of the international scene.

In addition, the arguments for the invasion advanced publicly by politicians frequently involved what seem to have been outright lies and complex deceptions. The Bush administration's linking of Saddam Hussein to the terrorist attacks on the USA of September 11, 2001 was one of the most conspicuous of these, but the massaging of intelligence reports by the British, Australian, and American regimes runs it a close second. Despite denials, the rationale for these seems to have been (at best) an amoral attitude to what would work politically.

This resort to mendacity brings us to a second example since it parallels the effective fear campaign waged so deceitfully in 2001 by the then Australian government in successfully painting asylum-seeking 'boat people' as demonic figures who had 'thrown their children overboard'. This portrait, created on the eve of an election in which opinion polls were forecasting defeat for the government, was palpably geared to frightening the electorate into staying with the 'safe' option of a long-serving conservative government and it proved an important factor in that government's winning re-election. Assuming that the conservative politicians believed their electoral survival had significant value for the community (and not just for their own careers), the case raises issues about the relation between the pursuit of power for good ends and the moral constraints on that.[1]

These two examples raise a number of questions about the relations between morality and politics, and these questions are at the heart of theoretical debates about what is called 'political realism'. This issue is addressed in Chapters 1 and 2. The examples also touch upon the related but significantly different problem of 'dirty hands' in politics to be addressed in Chapter 4.

My third case concerns the problem of armed humanitarian intervention. Consider someone who is dedicated both to the elimination or vast reduction of war and to a world in which injustice and persecution by states of their own citizens are abolished or greatly lessened. What stand can she make when faced with the demand for military intervention to prevent outrages like ethnic cleansing? There are various ways of phrasing the dilemma she faces, but one that has particular salience is in terms of a conflict of ideals: the ideal of peace in tension with the ideal of justice. Of course, it may well be that in particular cases the conflict is spurious. Often enough, resort to military power will simply and even predictably make the situation worse, in either the short or longer term, and, by contrast, there may be some rare cases in which armed intervention is so bloodless as to constitute no threat to peace. Nonetheless, some situations, such as the horrible slaughter in Rwanda

---

[1] For a detailed and depressing account of the Howard government's manipulations of the truth in these matters, see David Marr and Marian Wilkinson, *Dark Victory: How a Government Lied Its Way to Political Triumph* (Crows Nest, NSW: Allen and Unwin, 2004).

in 1994, appear to be those exceptional cases where 'war for humanity' to prevent the slaughter may make sense.[2] This case raises sharply a more general issue about the nature and role of ideals in politics, and this forms the subject matter of Chapter 3.

Moreover, the proponents of armed humanitarian intervention can face some of the problems of moralism discussed in Chapters 1 and 2, since enthusiasm for 'militant humanitarianism' (as some have called it) is prone to several of the forms of moralistic distortion there examined.[3] These problems, as well as those posed by the clash of ideals, confront people on the left (to use this much-degraded term as a broad brush indicator) who would not have supported the invasion of Iraq for reasons of realpolitik, and who recognize the falsehood and even dishonesty of the primary reasons given at the time for the invasion, but who think that it could be justified as a humanitarian action, citing the need to put an end to Saddam's record of human rights violations. There are of course grave doubts about retrospective 'justifications' for wars that were not justified that way at the time, and indeed were conducted by leaders who explicitly denied that such reasons could have been legitimate.[4] Even more importantly, the judgement that 'something must be done', so common in the argument for humanitarian intervention, often disregards the feasibility constraints on serious moral action, as the (in my view) eminently foreseeable, continuing chaos in Iraq seems to demonstrate.

My fourth case concerns the bombing campaigns against enemy cities practised by both Allied and Axis powers in World War II, and of course by other parties in other conflicts before and since. These campaigns were advocated for their efficacy in winning the war even

---

[2] For my reservations about enthusiasm for armed humanitarian intervention see C. A. J. Coady, 'War for Humanity: A Critique', in Deen K. Chatterjee and Don Scheid (eds.), *Ethics and Foreign Intervention* (Cambridge: Cambridge University Press, 2002), and *The Ethics of Armed Humanitarian Intervention*, Peaceworks 45 (Washington DC: United States Institute of Peace, 2002).

[3] One critic who uses the term 'militant humanitarianism' is Conor Gearty in his *Can Human Rights Survive?* (Cambridge: Cambridge University Press, 2006), 134.

[4] Most conspicuous was the Australian Prime Minister, Mr John Howard, who declared: 'I would have to accept that if Iraq had genuinely disarmed, I couldn't justify on its own a military invasion of Iraq to change the regime', only to later reassure the Australian troops at Tindal Air Base in the Northern Territory: 'You went in our name in a just cause; you were properly sent to liberate an oppressed people, and with your coalition partners you did that job magnificently and in a way that will always be remembered.' Transcripts are available online. See <www.pm.gov.au/media/speech/2003/speech74.cfm> and <www.pm.gov.au/media/speech/2003/speech95.cfm>.

though they violated existing understandings of what sort of targeting was morally permissible in war. Some of this advocacy was based on mere hatred, but much of it had an instrumental justification. Its advocates thought that the killing and maiming of thousands upon thousands of non-combatants (or 'innocents' in a slightly technical sense) including babies and children was justified by its contribution to winning the war. In the campaign against Germany alone, it is plausibly estimated (though estimates vary) that about 500,000 civilians were killed, and a comparable figure is given for the fire-bombing and nuclear bombing of Japan (though again, estimates vary).[5] Assuming that it was good to win the war, which was plausible in the case of the Allies (though the thought was available as subjective belief to both sides), then the question arises about the relation of this justification to the significance and strength of the moral objections to killing those who had done nothing to justify being attacked. Those who think morality somehow irrelevant to international politics, especially to war, will see the moral criticism of the slaughter of hundreds of thousands of non-combatants as beside the point. But even many of those who do not reject the significance of moral restraints on the conduct of war will nonetheless argue that some of these intentional attacks upon the innocent are permissible, even though they also think them in some sense immoral. This again raises the problem of dirty hands that is discussed in Chapter 4.

These examples are horrendous enough, and much of my discussion in what follows is concerned with the relation of morality to political decisions that directly affect major matters of life and death. But the topic of morality and politics can be pressing in less dramatic ways, as when people wonder whether the exercise of political power is compatible with ordinary integrity: whether, for instance, the necessary subordination of individual conscience to party discipline or the need to win power does

---

[5] Michael Clodfelter estimates 499,750 German and 299,485 Japanese civilian deaths as a result of Allied fire-bombing, and a further 78,150 and (at least) 23,753 casualties as a result of the atomic bombing of Hiroshima and Nagasaki respectively. See *Warfare and Armed Conflicts: A Statistical Reference to Casualty and Other Figures, 1500–1999* (Jefferson, NC: McFarland, 2002), 543; 580–1. Other authorities give much higher figures. It is worth recalling that the horrors of World War II produced no inhibition on city bombing. In the 'forgotten war' of Korea, the United States engaged in saturation bombing of all major North Korean cities and most of its towns with devastating effect. Curtis LeMay, head of US Strategic Air Command at the time, later boasted: 'we burned down just about every city in North and South Korea both . . . We killed off over a million civilian Koreans and drove several million more from their homes.' Quoted in Gregory Elich, 'Targeting North Korea', *Z Magazine* (31 December 2002), available online at <www.zmag.org/elich_korea.htm>, 30 January 2007.

not produce a disfigurement of character, a sort of pretence to honesty that verges on hypocrisy, and certainly, commonly enough, evokes the charge, and creates a mood, of cynicism. This problem is related to a specific problem with democratic politics, namely, whether it is possible to work for good in public life and maintain one's ideals when the power to do that work is dependent on the ephemeral and often corrupted forces of public opinion. The befuddled state of leftist parties (where they still exist) in many Western democracies is a testament to the power of this problem, and the problem was dramatically on display in the US presidential elections of 2004 where fear of the electorate's largely irrational attitudes to the war on terror drove the Democratic candidate, and most of his party, into support for the war in Iraq. Indeed, where disagreement with the President on this matter was aired at all, it consisted in calling for an injection of more US troops which amounted to a demand for escalation of the conflict, though with the hope that this would eventually improve the situation. A full discussion of these issues is beyond the scope of this short book, but some aspects of them are dealt with in Chapters 1, 2, and 3, and they are pertinent to the discussion in Chapter 5.

1

Morality, Moralism, and Realism

> And why beholdest thou the mote that is in thy brother's eye, but
> considerest not the beam that is in thine own eye?
>
> Matthew 7: 3 (King James Version)

There may have been a time, perhaps at the peak of Victorian self-esteem
in the English-speaking countries, when morality generally occupied an
unquestioned place at the top of a hierarchy of social and personal values.
Indeed, as the high tide of Christian religious influence began to ebb in
Europe, morality itself as a sort of institution began to supplant religion
and to exercise a bold and forthright role as the guide to life, if not the
object of worshipful respect. There was an Oxford B.Phil. examination
question in my first years at Oxford that quoted Wordsworth in his
'Ode to Duty' describing duty as the 'stern daughter of the voice of
God' and asked 'Why God?'. It seems likely that many answered there
was no need of God but accepted that morality remained a stern voice
(and I suspect some thought it still female, though more a mother
or a nanny than a daughter). Dostoyevsky's despairing thought in the
cry of Ivan Karamazov that 'without God, everything is permitted'
was certainly one response to the religious crisis of the nineteenth
century, but the more widespread response amongst most intellectuals
was to elevate rather than abandon morality, and to give a secular
status to its prescriptions. If it was thought to need a parent, then the
parent was likely to be Reason or even, absurdly enough, Society or
the State.

Traditionally indeed, any such elevation of morality had always
encountered doubters. Hume, of course, in his theoretical, sceptical
moods, but his doubts were not meant to have practical consequences,
and, like the ancient sceptics, Hume's doubts were wider than the arena
of morality. Earlier, Machiavelli very significantly tried to drive a wedge
between morality and the political concern for the distinctively public

good, and Nietzsche most dramatically of all tried to cast conventional morality as a crutch for the weak, an impediment to full self-respect. But it is in our own day, that more widespread theoretical doubts have arisen about morality's lofty standing, and even about what it, and its reflection in moral theorizing, could really amount to. Bernard Williams has been one of the most prominent in raising such doubts, going so far as to adapt the American description of slavery as a 'peculiar institution' to the characterization of morality itself. But he is one voice amongst many in what has sometimes been called the anti-morality, anti-moral theory movement amongst philosophers. I recall Gilbert Ryle saying long before this movement got under way: 'Moral philosophy's not only in the melting pot, it's in it upside down.'

I do not aim to solve, or even directly address, these debates in this book. I mention them merely to provide a background to what I shall try to do. This is a background that puts morality in a prominent place but makes its contours vague and somewhat ambiguous. People are still strongly moved by appeals to morality in both their private and public lives, and reasonably secure in their moral judgements across a range of circumstances, even if there remain areas that are highly contentious both in respect of high theory and concrete practical judgement. My principal focus will be on what remains, or should remain, of morality's place in the assessment of politics—what is done by political actors, proclaimed by policies, and enacted by governments—and, particularly, the assessment of those political performances that tend to wreak the most havoc in terms of the destruction and distortion of human life and of the normalcy of the world we live in, namely, the resort to political violence. In today's world, the role of morality has assumed a paradoxical aspect concerning the exercise of political violence, especially in view of the background sketched above. The paradox is at once both theoretical and practical. Theoretical, in that the attempts by a variety of intellectual fashions to dethrone morality's pretensions are confronted by more and more resort to moral terminology by the world's activists and political leaders: this is evident in the extraordinary growth in currency of 'human rights' discourse and the frequent invocation of just war theory. Practical, in that the brutal (even brutish) resort to force, unconstrained in reality by seriously moral, legal, or even prudential considerations, has been a striking feature of so much of the international order in the early years of the third millennium, even after the discourse of human rights and commitment to them has had remarkable triumphs, such as the velvet revolutions in Eastern Europe and the capitulation of the South African apartheid regime, to name only two of the most striking cases.

In this chapter I want to explore these issues further with particular reference to a certain style of denial of the relevance of morality to politics, especially international politics, and I will use the concept of moralism, and an account of it that I have developed elsewhere, to illustrate the general issues and to exhibit both the merits and defects of that style of denial. The style in question is best captured by the label 'political realism' which refers both to a particular intellectual school and to a mood amongst many politicians and political commentators. The theory of political realism was for many decades in the twentieth century immensely influential in academic circles, especially in the disciplines of political science and international relations. Moreover, it has had a direct influence on political policy through those of its proponents, like Henry Kissinger, George Kennan, and Jeane Kirkpatrick, who left academia to work in the highest levels of government. In the past twenty years or so its influence has waned somewhat, and there are at least three significant causes for that change. The first, already noted briefly above, is the influence of the human rights movement which has cast a distinctively moral light upon the misery and violations caused by governments principally to their own subjects, but also to other peoples. The second, which has complex connections to the first, is the revival of moral thinking about international politics amongst many intellectuals and academics, most notably philosophers. It would be unwise of a philosopher to succumb too greatly to the hubristic thought that his discipline has had some immediate effect upon the world of practical affairs, but that it has had a distinct influence in some of these affairs is more than plausible. In particular, the revival of just war thinking (and modifications of and resistance to it), the popularity of a confidently altruistic utilitarianism, and the influence of John Rawls's theory of justice, especially attempts to extend it beyond the merely local provenance that Rawls himself had initially given it, have all combined to make a moral assessment of political decisions, especially in the international arena, less eccentric than it had seemed during the heyday of realism. The third factor has been the revived influence of fundamentalist religious thinking which tends to see the arena of world and local politics through a very simple lens of good and evil, virtue and vice. This revival has many interesting, and indeed several alarming, aspects, but one crucial thing it has done, in both its Eastern and Western forms, is remind us that it is hard to make a sharp division between religion and politics, simply because most religions contain guides to and incentives for moral behaviour. These guides and incentives will inevitably play some part in the outlook on politics that is adopted by adherents. The liberal enterprise of attempting to check the more violent and dangerous tendencies of such outlooks is a noble one, and it has had remarkable successes, though it would be a mistake to imagine that only religious outlooks are subject to such tendencies to excess. In any case, the importance of such achievements as the separation of church and state, the abolition of religious tests for public office, and the insistence on freedom of religion should not have blinded the supporters of those achievements (as it too often did) to the influence that religious conviction will often have for thinking about political activity in moral terms.

So the current position with regard to politics and morality is complex and very interesting. The spirit of realism is still influential, especially in political science and some international relations circles, and the conflict between it and other approaches has something to teach. Indeed, my view is that realism itself, despite its flaws, has something to teach, especially because of the advance of some of its moral and religious rivals. As we shall, see, the realist outlook is itself deeply ambiguous. It is normally understood both by many supporters and opponents as the view that morality has no place in foreign affairs, or, sometimes, more generally in politics. In this form, it is regularly rebutted by philosophers, but the rebuttals have little effect upon its adherents, suggesting at least the possibility that the opponents on both sides are missing at least some of the point.[1] I shall draw upon the discussion of moralism to make it clearer what the debate should be about and how it might be resolved. In any case, the phenomenon of moralism is of interest in itself, and has implications for other areas of philosophy and for an understanding of some of the widespread doubts about the importance of morality itself. Indeed, one rather dyspeptic intellectual has gone so far as to claim that moralism is nowadays rampant in our culture. 'It is hard to think', John Kekes tells us, 'of any area of life that is free of the exhortation of one or another group of moralizers.'[2] And here the term 'moralizer' is not

---

[1] Two of the most perceptive of these philosophical critiques are those of Charles Beitz, *Political Theory and International Relations* (Princeton: Princeton University Press, 1979), and Robert Holmes, *On War and Morality* (Princeton: Princeton University Press, 1989), ch. 2.

[2] John Kekes, 'On the Supposed Obligation to Relieve Famine', *Philosophy*, 77 (2002), 503.

intended to be flattering. Nor is the term 'moral' intended as praise in Charles Dickens's splendid portrait of a moralizer in the figure of Saul Pecksniff in *Martin Chuzzlewit*:

It has been remarked that Mr. Pecksniff was a moral man. So he was. Perhaps there never was a more moral man than Mr. Pecksniff: especially in his conversations and correspondence . . . He was a most exemplary man: fuller of virtuous precept than a copybook. Some people likened him to a direction-post, which is always telling the way to a place, and never goes there: but these were his enemies; the shadows cast by his brightness; that was all. His very throat was moral.[3]

But more of moralism later. Let me turn now to some clarifications of realism. Realists often complain that their critics distort, even caricature, their position, but this is at least in part a function of the diversity of the things affirmed as basic to their outlook by different (or even the same) realists and of the consequent opacity created by the uncertain relation between these things. Lest it seem that the difficulty is wholly in the eye of an unrealistic philosophical beholder of the landscape of political science, it may be worth noting the agreement of so eminent a political scientist as Stanley Hoffmann. 'The first problem', Hoffmann said of realism, 'is its essential elasticity and indeterminateness.'[4]

WHAT IS THE REALIST CRITIQUE OF MORALITY?

We should begin by distinguishing realism as a theoretical construct from mere rationalizations of the brutal practices that states often engage in, especially when at war. There may indeed be certain connections between the two, but, despite the ambiguities of realist thinking, the simplistic amoralism of the justifications offered to support the vicious Athenian sacking of Melos, for instance, differ in structure and spirit from the analyses offered by many of the theorists we are to consider.[5]

---

[3] *The Life and Adventures of Martin Chuzzlewit* (London: Oxford University Press, 1951), 12–13. I am grateful to Robert Fullinwider for drawing my attention to this passage.

[4] Stanley Hoffmann, *World Disorders: Troubled Peace in the Post-Cold War Era* (Lanham: Rowman & Littlefield, 1998), 59.

[5] Michael Walzer's well-known treatment of what he calls 'realism' in chapter 1 of *Just and Unjust Wars* is somewhat misleading in this respect. He concentrates upon Thucydides' account of the arguments for the vicious sacking of Melos, and links that with parts of Hobbes's outlook on war, but makes no reference there to the academic

Nonetheless, although the articulations of realism express more than a naked commitment to 'might is right', the ambiguities in those articulations suggest that its adherents are less united by some central doctrine than by an outlook, or even an intellectual mood. There are certain respects in which what it most resembles is a religion, especially in view of the moral passion with which its apparent denunciations of morality are pursued. Religion and realism share many features, such as, the combination of an often loosely related set of beliefs, a common style of thinking and responding, a sometimes desperate desire to preach to the uncomprehending heathen, and a pantheon of canonical exemplars or saints whose very diverse intellectual and practical lives are seen to embody the virtues of the religion. Like many religions it has its sects ('neo-realism', 'structural realism', etc.) and its schools of doctrinal interpretation, and just as the rival Christian theological schools can sometimes seem further apart from one another than from atheists, so too with contending interpreters of realism and its demands as evidenced by the dramatic oppositions of George Kennan and Henry Kissinger on Vietnam, or Morgenthau and Nitze on nuclear weapons, or the gulf between Niebhur and Waltz on theoretical matters like the foundations of the 'science' of international relations. Hoffmann notes this sort of difference as 'striking' and 'a little disturbing'. Again, in spite of their fulminations against various appeals to morality in foreign affairs, there is a moral passion about much realist writing that tends to reinforce the religious analogy I have suggested. Indeed, one author who has written a sympathetic account of several key realist thinkers called his book, *Righteous Realists.*[6]

I make this religious analogy in no spirit of disparagement, and certainly with no suggestion that the doctrines and spirit of realism should not be taken seriously. In fact there are certain insights in realism that seem to me to be essentially right, but they are often obscured by the rhetorical, polemical, and interpretive processes within realism itself. One thing I hope to do here is to make them more transparent, and in the course of doing so move the debates about ethics in foreign affairs

tradition that embraces the term 'realism'. Later in the book, he has a brief discussion of it and exempts it from implication in the Thucydian realism discussed in chapter 1. Walzer, *Just and Unjust Wars: A Moral Argument with Historical Illustrations*, 3rd edn. (New York: Basic Books, 2000).

[6] Joel H. Rosenthal, *Righteous Realists: Political Realism, Responsible Power, and American Culture in the Nuclear Age* (Baton Rouge and London: Louisiana State University Press, 1991).

beyond some of the sterility that often surrounds the stark oppositions of realism and idealism.

The realists' litany of saints is a long and venerable one, dating back at least to Thucydides and St Augustine, and including along the way Machiavelli, Hobbes, Max Weber, E. H. Carr, Reinhold Niebuhr, Hans Morgenthau, George Kennan, Dean Acheson, and Henry Kissinger. Indeed, some realists, like some religious, have a very expansive, ecumenical sense of their saintly antecedents; one list includes as well as St Augustine, 'John Calvin, Edmund Burke, James Madison, and most other classical Western thinkers'.[7] When we survey the rich diversity of thought and attitude encompassed by even those figures on the more restricted list and scores of lesser lights, it is tempting to despair of the prospect of discovering any unity of belief and stance amongst them. But I think it is worth spelling out some strands that might bind this diverse group together even if the strands do criss-cross in the way Wittgenstein had in mind when he spoke of concepts that were united by overlapping strands of family resemblance. Here are five such elements:

1. a certain opposition to idealism and morality in foreign affairs;
2. an opposition to moral self-inflation;
3. a concern for the national interest as a focal value for foreign policy;
4. a concern for stability in the international order;
5. a concern for close attention to the realities of power.

All of these can be abundantly illustrated from realist writings. So can a certain amount of confusion about what each of them means or entails. Arthur Schlesinger Jr.'s brilliant and provocative paper 'The Necessary Amorality of Foreign Affairs' is instructive here, especially about 1 and 2 above.[8] (I shall have more to say about 3, 4, and 5 later, but how they are understood and supported must hinge on our interpretation of 1 and 2.) His article is principally a stinging indictment of the Vietnam war, but it also objects to the moral stances of some opponents of the war. Schlesinger thinks that foreign relations are actually *somehow* beyond morality (hence his title) but concedes rather nervously that morality cannot be banished entirely from the subject.

---

[7] Ernest W. Lefever, *Moralism and US Foreign Policy* (Washington DC: The Brookings Institution, 1973), 397.

[8] Arthur Schlesinger, 'The Necessary Amorality of Foreign Affairs', *Harper's Magazine* (Aug. 1971).

Hence his strongest denunciations of the intrusion of morality are often followed by qualifications. So we find him posing and answering a question about the matter as follows, 'Should—as both supporters and critics of the Indochina war have asserted—overt moral principles decide issues of foreign policy? Required to give a succinct answer, I am obliged to say: as little as possible.' But then he adds, 'Moral values in international politics . . . should be decisive only in questions of last resort. One must add that questions of last resort do exist.'[9] Later, he says: 'The raw material of foreign affairs is, most of the time, morally neutral or ambiguous. In consequence, for the great majority of foreign-policy transactions, moral principles cannot be decisive.'[10] Later he allows nonetheless that 'an irrespressible [*sic*] propensity to moral judgement in the field of foreign affairs exists. Nor despite the perils of moral absolutism, is it without value.'[11] Similar uncertainties can be culled from other notable realists. The influential American realist Hans Morgenthau is anxious to separate politics from morality by maintaining 'the autonomy of the political sphere'. He recognizes the autonomy of other spheres such as economics, law, and morality, but insists that the political realist must 'subordinate these other standards to those of politics'.[12] Yet part of what he takes to be essential to realism is that it 'refuses to identify the moral aspirations of a particular nation with the moral laws that govern the universe'.[13] This looks like an acknowledgement that there are such 'laws' and that they govern politics, as all else, but Morgenthau then insists that this general acknowledgement should be set against the quite other thing by which nations are tempted, namely 'to pretend to know with certainty what is good and evil in the relations among nations'.[14] So it seems to be a sort of presumption to moral knowledge that Morgenthau rejects. Again, E. H. Carr, one of the few non-American writers claimed in the modern realist canon, furiously denounces various dangers of resort to morality in foreign affairs, and characterizes a basic conflict therein as that between realism and utopianism. Nonetheless, he is unequivocal in his belief that there is a place for morality and idealism in foreign policy, saying, 'Utopia and reality are thus the two facets of political science. Sound political thought and sound political life will be found

---

[9] Ibid. 72.   [10] Ibid. 73.   [11] Ibid. 75.

[12] Hans J. Morgenthau, *Politics Among Nations: The Struggle for Power and Peace*, 7th edn. (Boston: McGraw-Hill Higher Education, 2006), 13.

[13] Ibid. 12.   [14] Ibid.

where both have their place.'[15] Later he states as 'the realist view' that 'no ethical standards are applicable to relations between states. . . '.[16] Later still, he refers to 'that uneasy compromise between power and morality which is the foundation of all political life'.[17] And in spite of his intermittent taste for a fairly simple version of moral relativism, he gives a significant and positive role to the operation of an understanding of 'grounds of justice' in international relations.[18] What are we to make of this? Is the realist position on the place of morality just a tissue of confusions?

Not just, though there are confusions aplenty. What I want to suggest is that realism is misunderstood, and sometimes misunderstands itself, as involving *any* sort of opposition to morality or ethics in international affairs. The realist target is, or should be, not morality but certain distortions of morality, distortions that deserve the name moralism. This is a name that they are sometimes given in realist writings, though often the word 'moralism' is used by realists as virtually synonymous with 'morality'. Indeed, it is the failure consistently to distinguish morality from moralism, and the associated absence of any sort of theory of moralism, that largely explains the curious convolutions about the role of morality that we have already noticed in the authors cited.[19] But that it is moralism and not morality that they attempt to exorcize is indicated by some of the specific targets that concern Schlesinger in his article. During his critique, he condemns not morality but a variety of what are surely distortions of it: 'moral absolutism', 'moral self-aggrandizement', 'superior righteousness', 'fanaticism', and 'excessive righteousness'.[20] Several of these are clearly vices, even if a precise account of their viciousness would need some spelling out. For instance, even the slightest sympathy with the Aristotelian theory of virtue as a

[15] Edward Hallett Carr, *The Twenty Year Crisis 1919–1939: An Introduction to the Study of International Relations* (London: MacMillan, 1962), 10.

[16] Ibid. 153.   [17] Ibid. 220.

[18] Ibid. Although Carr is often taken to be a realist, he is perhaps better seen as a 'fellow traveller' of realism. He is sympathetic to what he takes realism to assert, but thinks it goes a little too far in leaving no place for 'utopian' ethics.

[19] Kenneth W. Thompson is one of the few who makes an explicit distinction between morality and moralism and gives a brief account of what the distinction might be. Citing Morgenthau and Kennan, he defines 'moralism' as 'the tendency to make one moral value supreme and to apply it indiscriminately without regard to time and place'. Thompson, *Moralism and Morality in Politics and Diplomacy: The Credibility of Institutions, Policies and Leadership* (Lanham: University Press of America, 1985), 5. As we shall see, this is far too simple, and possibly misleading, an account of moralism.

[20] Schlesinger, 'The Necessary Amorality', 73–5.

mean between opposite excesses would count excessive righteousness and moral self-aggrandizement as vicious, and no person who regards him or herself as moral would accept cheerfully the description 'fanatic'. The epithets 'superior righteousness' and 'moral absolutism' need a bit more discussion, but it is surely open to us to treat them as indicating ways in which morality is distorted rather than standard features of it. The same conclusion is suggested by perusal of other realist arguments. Raymond Aron, for instance, says, 'The criticism of idealist illusion is not only pragmatic, it is also moral. Idealist diplomacy slips too often into fanaticism.'[21] Clearly, this is a moral objection to a false use of morality. In Aron's case, he associates the distortion of morality with a certain kind of idealism. In Morgenthau's, it is partly a matter of misplaced epistemic certainty.

It would, I am confident, be possible to bring in evidence vastly more citations from contemporary realist writers and classical 'saints' to support my contention that it is moralism rather than morality that is most plausibly viewed as the target of realist critique. But the more urgent task is to spell out the outlines of a concept of moralism that will make sense of realism as a critical apparatus directed at certain sorts of misguided appeals to morality. This should directly illuminate strands 1 and 2 listed above and indirectly cast light upon 3, 4, and 5.

Our task is complicated by the fact that the topic of moralism is radically under-explored in moral philosophy, though several recent developments have made inroads on what seems to be the same or a similar project without use of the term 'moralism', so I can do no more than begin work on an adequate account here; nonetheless, the sketch that follows should be sufficient for the purpose of shedding light on what is true and what is not in realism.

MORALISM: ITS VARIETIES AND THE QUESTION OF SCOPE

Moralism is a kind of vice involved in certain ways of practising morality or exercising moral judgement, or thinking that you are doing so. It is a vice that seems to have been unknown to the ancients. Indeed, until quite recently, terms like 'moralize', 'moralizer', and 'moralism'

---

[21] Raymond Aron, *Peace and War: A Theory of International Relations*, trans. Richard Howard and Annette Baker Fox (Garden City, NY: Doubleday, 1966), 307.

would not have been used with the negative connotations they now universally have. For 'moralism', the *Oxford English Dictionary* lists its earliest use as 1828 and the entry on 'moralize' (in my 1959 edition of the *Shorter OED*) contains no account at all of a pejorative use of the expression. One finds nothing like it in Aristotle's close and subtle discussion of virtues and vices, and in some respects this is rather surprising. But perhaps we need something like the circumstances of the post-Christian world that has emerged since the late eighteenth century to appreciate fully the phenomenon to which the word 'moralism' points. By characterizing our world as 'post-Christian' I do not mean to suggest that Christianity is no longer relevant to our world, nor that Christian faith is no longer a genuine option for contemporary life, but rather that the removal of Christianity from the openly dominant position it had exercised in Western social and political life for so many centuries has major implications for the nature of civil and political life, for moral and political discourse, and for the understanding of such terms as secular, profane, holy, and religious. Indeed, there seems to me to be a sense in which Christianity provides some of the materials for the very understanding of moralism as a vice, for instance in Christ's injunction to 'judge not that ye be not judged' and in the advice to attend to obstructions in one's own eye before pointing to those in the eyes of others. The idea that only God can really judge the state of soul of anyone and hence the appropriateness of a certain modesty and even apprehension about one's own spiritual standing and destiny may have moved from a theological setting to a more this-worldly one during the advance of secularization. Yet it is also true that the deep divisions of belief and unbelief characteristic of so many modern societies provide a fresh challenge to the role of moral judgement in political and social life. If it is against this background that the current frequency of the resort to charges of moralism should be viewed, the widespread use of the expression and its relatives seems inversely proportional to the clarity of our understanding of what it means. It is therefore ripe for a philosophical investigation.[22] In this chapter, I will begin such an analysis and continue it in the next chapter.

Initially, there seem to be two sides to the vice of moralism: inappropriate attitudes or emotions and inappropriate actions. Commonly enough the two go together but some criticisms of moralism concentrate

[22] For a concerted attempt at such an exploration see the essays in C. A. J. Coady (ed.), *What's Wrong with Moralism?* (Oxford: Blackwell, 2006).

more on one rather than the other, and it is possible for someone to do the right thing in the wrong spirit. In broad terms, we can say that the vice of moralism often involves an inappropriate set of emotions or attitudes in making or acting upon moral judgements, or in judging others in the light of moral considerations. The moralizer is typically thought to lack self-awareness and a breadth of understanding of others and of the situations in which she and they find themselves. In addition, or in consequence, the moralizer is subject to an often-delusional sense of moral superiority over those coming under his or her judgement. Though these character traits are commonly associated with moralism, the vice needs to be specified in terms of its typical ways of working and so needs to be distinguished, for instance, from the related vice of hypocrisy. Nonetheless, it seems unlikely that moralism will take one simple form. Beginning in this chapter and continuing in Chapter 2, I will offer and explore a preliminary typology as a suitable beginning for analysis, though a fully developed theory may require its modification, and there is, in any event, a degree of overlap between the categories. My classifications will involve six types of moralism: moralism of scope, moralism of unbalanced focus, moralism of imposition or interference, moralism of abstraction, absolutist moralism, and moralism of deluded power. In spelling these out, I will indicate the ways in which the preoccupations of realist thinkers bear, accurately or inaccurately, upon each category. In this chapter, I will concentrate upon moralism of scope and its relevance to the concerns of realism.

Moralism of scope involves seeing things as moral issues that aren't, and thereby overmoralizing the universe. A variation on this is the tendency to see minor moral matters as major ones or to collapse certain pertinent spheres of morality into other, more demanding ones, so that the morally advisable becomes the morally obligatory, or the somewhat morally preferable becomes a stern duty. I once had a colleague who made staff meetings almost impossible by the tendency to detect deep moral issues in every item of business. Even the simplest question of efficient practice was transformed into an issue of justice and rights. Sometimes there were moral dimensions to our decisions, but they concerned what was, on the whole, morally preferable rather than what was palpably morally demanded. Most of us have experienced some version of this phenomenon. Someone who views too many issues and decisions as richly moral ones may well merit the description (in the *OED* definition of moralism) 'addicted to moralizing' where 'moralizing' is given its old, non-pejorative sense of the bringing of a moral dimension to bear upon events, actions, or works of art. In true Aristotelian fashion the vice consists of an excess on a mean (the contrary vice would be an insufficient inclination to make such judgements, though I am not sure that we have a word for it.)

This kind of criticism raises acutely questions about the boundaries of morality and morality's claims to dominance and comprehensiveness. There is a clear connection here with some of the concerns of realists, and an echo of Machiavelli's strictures on the inappropriateness of some moral judgements and virtues to much of the conduct required of a Prince, both in his dealings with subjects and with other Princes. (I do not want to endorse the specifics of Machiavelli's critique since I think that a good deal of it is mistaken; the form of his objections, however, illustrates my point about this type of moralism.) A weak version of the scope restriction is the view that there are many matters that are too trivial for direct moral concern: whether to go to this movie or that, whether to exercise by swimming or walking—these are the sorts of things that it would usually be foolish to bring within the purview of morality (though there may be contexts in which they could have moral significance). An excessive concern for the sway of morality can bring with it crippling psychological attitudes that themselves damage the operation of moral judgement. This has been recognized in the tradition of Christian moral theology by the use of the term 'scrupulosity' to refer to the condition where someone is given to damaging self-doubt as a result of excessive worry about whether various, basically minor and harmless pursuits are morally wrong. I dare say other spiritual and religious traditions have recognized the same defect and given it an appropriate name. Such people have 'scruples' in a theologically and morally pejorative sense because their worry and concern inhibit their moral growth and paralyse healthy action. (The word 'scruple' in ordinary language is interestingly two-faced since it has something of this negative sense, but also has a positive sense in which it is, for example, a criticism to say that someone has no scruples.) It is tempting to think that moralism is a vice that only arises in the delivery of moral judgements upon others, and this is certainly a common arena for its appearance. But the example of scrupulosity shows that moralism of scope can be self-directed: the scrupulous are moralistic about themselves.

A stronger version of the restriction of the scope of morality's claims challenges either the comprehensiveness of morality and/or its dominance with respect to matters that are both intrinsically important and amenable to reason. One version of this restriction is the claim that there may be rational demands that not only conflict with morality but override it. This brings us into some very deep waters that are, for my purposes here, best avoided; in particular, it touches on the debate about 'dirty hands' which has some relevance to realism (and to Machiavelli), and I intend to return to this topic in Chapter 3. In any case, I think it better to construe the dirty hands debate as a controversy about conditions of extremity (the politician 'must' order the torture of a terrorist's child to find out the whereabouts of a bomb that threatens other innocent lives) and the realist concerns about politics and morality are as much related to significant but quotidian policy as to such dramatic emergencies.[23] A further point of difference is that dirty hands decisions are usually characterized as those that involve a violation of morality that still remains pertinent to the decision and to the agent's consciousness of what she has done and what she has become. Realists are inclined to dismiss or downplay the relevance of morality in a way that dirty hands theorists are not. The difference can be explained by invoking the ideas of dominance and comprehensiveness mentioned earlier. These express somewhat different pictures of the status of morality, though an exalted understanding of morality often draws on both. Morality's dominance would consist in its trumping all other considerations whenever it is relevant to them at all, whereas morality's comprehensiveness consists in its being universally relevant whether it trumps other considerations or not. Dirty hands theorists accept morality's comprehensiveness (at least with respect to the domains they are concerned with) but reluctantly reject its dominance for one class of decisions; political realists are often viewed (and often present themselves) as cheerfully rejecting the comprehensive relevance of morality by reference to something special about politics or international relations.

In this connection, realists often appeal to the idea that some moral concerns are rendered irrelevant by the rational dictates of prudence. This makes a point of connection with the realist theme that morality sometimes (or commonly) demands the impossible of international policy and ignores the realities of power; it also connects with the

---

[23] It should be noted, however, that there are those that dissent from the view that 'dirty hands' problems arise only in extreme situations. See e.g. Michael Stocker, 'Dirty Hands and Ordinary Life', in Paul Rynard and David P. Shugarman (eds.), *Cruelty and Deception: The Controversy over Dirty Hands in Politics* (Peterborough, Ontario: Broadview Press; Australia: Pluto Press, 2000), 27–42. This is a version of his chapter 1 in *Plural and Conflicting Values* (Oxford: Oxford University Press, 1990).

common realist opposition between concern for national self-interest and morality. It is plausible to suppose that one restriction on the scope of morality is that imposed by the acknowledgement that what morality apparently demands is impossible. As Stanley Hoffmann puts it: 'a deontological ethic in which the definition of what is right is not derived from a calculation of what is possible condemns itself to irrelevance if its commands cannot be carried out in the world as it is'.[24] Building on this sort of insight, realists link it to the advocacy of national interest as the primary rationale for international relations. Expecting nations to put morality ahead of national interest is, in some sense, expecting the impossible.

Morality should certainly be attentive to circumstance and the way it conditions what is possible. The slogan 'ought implies can', though open to a number of interpretations and exceptions, certainly reminds us of the futility of demanding what is totally impossible in the circumstances, however fine it may be elsewhere. Reasoning with people over disagreements is a good thing, but urging us to reason with an attacking homicidal maniac usually has no point; either flight or forceful defence, if available options, makes much more sense. The imperative of prudence is overwhelming.

This is not to say that the relationship of morality to possibility or impossibility is straightforward. There is a case for holding that certain moral demands are not rendered irrelevant or null and void by contingencies that make it difficult or even impossible to implement them. G. A. Cohen, for one, has argued forcefully that facts of any sort are irrelevant to moral principles.[25] People may indeed sometimes be excused violation of moral principles where they are coerced or otherwise powerless to conform, but the principles stand nonetheless. Slavery was unjust (my example) even when it was well entrenched, part of normal economic operations, and thought impossible to eliminate. We don't want the validity of our moral principles to turn on such facts as these.

There is too much involved in this debate for it to be addressed at length here, but two points of clarification may be sketched. The first is that the idea of 'a moral principle' can be misleadingly broad for

---

[24] Hoffmann, *World Disorders*, 152. Hoffmann's statement of the point, however, tends to elide two different issues: the way in which moral injunctions are grounded or derived and the feasibility of applying them in current circumstances.

[25] G. A. Cohen, 'Facts and Principles', *Philosophy and Public Affairs*, 31/3 (2003), 211–45.

the purposes of my discussion of moralism and realism. It can cover hard-core moral prohibitions such as that against intentional killing of the innocent or against torture, but it can also cover injunctions like 'justice requires fair distribution of resources' or quasi-legal principles like 'no one should be condemned without an opportunity to confront their accusers'. It may also cover things that plausibly fall under the heading of ideals, such as the moral ideals of peace or social justice, which is the topic to be addressed directly in Chapter 3. It is not likely that the way facts bear or fail to bear upon the validity of all such 'principles' will be the same. Second, Cohen's primary concern is with the validity of moral principles, whereas mine is primarily with their implementation. As we shall see most clearly in the case of ideals, an ideal may remain valid even in circumstances that make it unfeasible or unwise to act in accordance with it. Even the justice principle about resources may require adjustment or at least strong reinterpretation in the face of certain facts to do with scarcity and the demands of prudence, as in triage situations where facts external to the worth of the agent may necessitate a skewing of resource distribution. Then there are the facts about political emergency that seem to require 'dirty hands' where a moral principle is said to retain its validity even though it 'must' be violated, an issue that will be addressed in Chapter 4.

Cohen's thesis is worth more discussion but I cannot pursue it further here, except to remark that not only is it somewhat tangential to my concerns in this book, but I remain unconvinced that even the validation of moral principles can be wholly independent of all facts. Were certain facts about human nature, for instance, quite different, it would surely affect the validity of moral principles: if human beings had a greatly reduced aversion to pain then the moral objections to torture would be quite different.

CLARIFYING SCOPE: PRUDENCE, MORALITY, AND THE NATIONAL INTEREST

Yet, for many of the situations envisaged by the realists, as indeed in the example of flight or defence, it is wrong to oppose morality and prudence. Any such opposition is complicated by different understandings of prudence. It is common in contemporary writings to treat prudence as something essentially to do with self-interest and thereby inherently hostile to the spirit of morality. But this stark contrast obscures too much. For one thing, a long tradition in moral philosophy and in ordinary thought views prudence as a part of morality, a moral virtue in its own right. In this light, prudence is not specifically concerned with the promotion and protection of self-interest, though it may encompass that. It is more a matter of moderation and of realistic appreciation in the exercise of practical judgement; indeed, on some accounts, it provides the very form of practical judgement. But we do not have to settle its exact delineation here. What is clear is that one may show imprudence, not only in dealing with one's own affairs, but in helping and advising others, and generally in dealing with their welfare. The tendency to misjudgement of consequences and circumstances that characterizes imprudence is wider than mere misjudgement of one's own interest. Adequate judging of the feasibility of action in these circumstances with these consequences, comprehending what is possible and what is not, should be part of any serious ethic, deontological or otherwise. Hoffman is right to insist upon this sort of prudence, but wrong to suggest that an ethic of rights and duties must ignore it.

The downgrading of prudent attention to likely outcomes that is consequent upon moralistic passion is discussed here under the heading of moralism of scope, but it has affinities with the moralism of abstraction to be examined later. However classified, it is a phenomenon that was clearly at work in the ill-fated invasion of Iraq. Those who promoted the necessity of the invasion paid scant attention to the likely outcomes, beyond those to be achieved on the initial battlefield. Their picture of the post-invasion scene in Iraq was distorted by occupancy of an illusory moral high ground from which the post-war environment was glimpsed through spectacles designed for the contemplation of values such as freedom, democracy, liberation from oppression, and gratitude to benefactors, but ill-suited to perceiving the realities of military occupation, the probable responses of displaced elites, the broader consequences of Western invasion of Middle Eastern countries, the likely stimulus to terrorism, and the probability that a secular dictatorship would give way to something like tribal and religious anarchy. The moral fervour with which some of the influential advocates of the invasion supported their case blinded them to the practicalities involved, even though, as I have argued, it should have been part of a genuine moral concern to take such practicalities and consequences more thoroughly into account. In this respect, moralism triumphed over morality to the detriment of us all, but especially of course, to the detriment of the people of Iraq.[26]

Moreover, as we have seen, the realistic appreciation of circumstances, empirical limitations, and consequences need give no particular pre-eminence to self-interest, in either its individual or national forms. Indeed, a sensible appreciation of the role of power in international affairs, an appreciation insisted on by realists, may require the prudent trimming of one's own interests. But even if prudence did have the narrow scope of concern for self-interest, it would not necessarily be opposed to morality. This is because, on some common ways of thinking about morality, an appropriate concern for one's own well-being is a legitimate part of it. As such, this concern may come into conflict with other moral demands, and needs to be seen as one thing amongst others conditioning what is possible in the circumstances of decision and policy. But this is not peculiar to it, since various other-directed moral concerns can equally come into conflict. Nor is there any reason to believe that even a legitimate concern for personal well-being must always trump other moral concerns. Sometimes it will be right to sacrifice our own advantage for that of others, notably, of course, though not exclusively, when the benefit to ourselves is slight and the benefit accruing to others is great. For all these reasons, the idea that it is somehow impossible to act against interest, either individual or national, must be rejected, even as we respect the relevance of possibility and demands of prudence.

Nor should we neglect the fact that there are often intimate connections between self-interest and a concern for the well-being of others. Certainly these concerns can conflict, but they are often in harmony. Those philosophers who thought that the general good and individual well-being were always at some deep level in agreement were probably too optimistic about the unity of morality and of self-interested rationality.[27] Nonetheless, the coincidence of such interests is a common enough fact, even when it needs some hard thinking to discover it. And the same is true of national and supranational interests. Just as an individual can have good self-centred reasons for promoting a general peace that benefits others (as Hobbes saw) so it will often be in the long-run interest of particular nations to promote international peace,

---

[26] A similarly unbalanced application of morality seems to have been partly responsible for the massive Israeli military reaction to the Hezbollah incursion into Israeli territory from Lebanon in July 2006.

[27] I am thinking here particularly of Plato in the *Republic* and rather differently of Hobbes in the *Leviathan*.

prosperity, and the reduction of world poverty. Realists are often tempted to a particularly short-sighted and narrow construal of the national interest.[28]

Against this, it might be urged that, in the international arena at least, there is no room for anything but self-interest, in the sense of national interest, because that arena is the dog-eat-dog scene approximating to Hobbes's description of the state of nature. Indeed, Hobbes, facing the question of the historical reality of his postulated state of nature, responded by admitting that it 'was never generally so over the whole world' but existed amongst the 'savage people' in America at that time and would exist wherever government collapsed into civil war.[29] He then famously gave the international order as an illustration of conditions at the level of sovereigns that mirrored the suspicion and hostility at the level of individuals that produced the state of nature. Hobbes does not say that the international order *is* a state of nature, but it involves a 'posture of war' that with individuals would produce such a state. National leaders are, he says, 'in continual jealousies and in the state and posture of gladiators, having their weapons pointing and their eyes fixed on one another, that is, their forts, garrisons, and guns upon the frontiers of their kingdoms, and continual spies upon their neighbours, which is a posture of war. But because they uphold thereby the industry of their subjects, there does not follow from it that misery which accompanies the liberty of particular men.'[30] Realists not only list Hobbes as a prominent 'saint', but often endorse his view of the international order. It must be allowed that Hobbes is a shrewd observer of human realities, and the depressing contemporary scale of standing armies, nuclear weapons, and sophisticated military technologies testifies to the permanent validity of his jaundiced view of the mutual mistrust and malevolence that disfigure international relations. This is not the place for a thorough exposition and critique of his views, but his picture clearly exaggerates the degree of hostility that obtains universally in the international order and leaves out much that softens the picture. For one thing, there are many states that do not stand in such a posture of war toward one another, for instance,

---

[28] A particularly good example of this narrowness can be found in Felix Oppenheim, *The Place of Morality in Foreign Policy* (Lexington, Mass.: Lexington Books, 1991). Oppenheim restricts national interests entirely to what he calls 'material benefits' such as territorial integrity (or political sovereignty), military security, and economic well-being.

[29] Thomas Hobbes, *Leviathan*, ch. 13 (London: Penguin Books, 1968), p. 187.

[30] Ibid. 187–8.

Australia and New Zealand, the United States and Canada, and most states in the European Union. No doubt, they spy on one another, sometimes as much for commercial advantage as for military secrets, but their weaponry is mostly aimed elsewhere. And the scope for moral interactions within the international order is clearly much greater than any picture derived from Hobbes would allow. This picture is heavily statist, but states are not today, and probably never were, the only actors in that order, and many other agents, such as international charities and other non-governmental agencies, are frequently motivated by palpable moral reasons in their behaviour. Moreover, they often interact with and are supported by states. States themselves act from a variety of mixed motives that often include compassionate motivations, as in disaster relief. Indeed, realists themselves often point out examples where states have acted at least partly from moral motives with, as they believe, deplorable results. (This is part of the prudential critique of moralism.) The drive to establish democratic governments in various parts of the world partly stems from a moral appreciation of the superiority of democracy over autocratic dictatorship, even where it also results from something less noble, like imperial ambition or an interest in secure markets. Of course, the scenario behind the Hobbesian state of nature does not require a total absence of moral motivations, but it does require that they are sufficiently rare to be rationally crushed by the dominance of other motivations. Glory hunters, power seekers, and the greedy are sufficiently numerous that self-preservation requires the stifling of all moral motivations but the most minimal (in family relations, for instance) and demands the mimicking of rapacious motivations, as in pre-emptive strikes. But even if this were true at the level of individuals (which I doubt), the relative security of the international order, even if it is more sporadic in some places than others, need not stifle moral motivations in the same way.

A more extreme version of the scope restriction can be found in the insistence by some theorists that politics and morality are distinct and autonomous realms of judgement and decision. This was the burden of one of Morgenthau's objections cited earlier when he referred to 'the autonomy of the political sphere' along with the autonomy of other domains such as economics, law, and morality, further insisting that the political realist must 'subordinate these other standards to those of politics'. Morgenthau's position is a striking echo of central themes in the work of the German conservative thinker Carl Schmitt by whom he was clearly influenced. Schmitt became embroiled with the Nazi Party in the 1930s and enjoyed (if that is the word) some fame for a time as a theoretician for the Nazi cause. Schmitt's thought has had a revival of sorts in recent years, so it is worth examining his position in detail.

Schmitt argues that the very definition of politics proceeds by reference to the notion of enemy. The 'specific political distinction to which political actions and motives can be reduced is that between friend and enemy', he claims.[31] This antithesis provides a criterion for politics that 'corresponds to the relatively independent criteria of other antitheses: good and evil in the moral sphere, beautiful and ugly in the aesthetic sphere, and so on'.[32] He also mentions elsewhere the profitable and unprofitable as a 'final distinction' in economics.[33] Defining enemies and dealing with them is the essential role of politics and it transcends the pretensions of 'universal' morality. Hence, the distinction friend/enemy is not merely a notable feature of politics for Schmitt, it transcends other considerations such as the moral. Schmitt allows for interactions between the other spheres and the political, so in principle there seems to be room for moral judgements within politics, but this concession has little real force in his outlook. All it does is allow moral considerations to be marshalled in support of the independently established political judgement. So Schmitt says: 'Emotionally the enemy is easily treated as being evil and ugly, because every distinction, most of all the political, as the strongest and most intense of the distinctions and categorizations, draws upon other distinctions for support. This does not alter the autonomy of such distinctions.'[34] In particular, the determination of friend/enemy and the decision to resort to violence against the enemy can have no reference to moral criteria independent of the will of the political leader. As Schmitt puts it, the distinction which has 'the utmost degree of intensity' exists 'theoretically and practically, without having simultaneously to draw upon all those moral, aesthetic, economic or other distinctions'.[35] The enemy is 'in a specially intense way, existentially something different and alien, so that in the extreme case conflicts with him are possible. These can neither be decided by a previously determined general norm nor by the judgement of a disinterested and therefore neutral third party.'[36]

Schmitt's is an extreme denial of the role of morality in politics, but even he finds it hard to banish the taint of morality entirely. In

---

[31] Carl Schmitt, *The Concept of the Political*, trans. George Schwab (New Brunswick NJ: Rutgers University Press, 1976), 26.
[32] Ibid.   [33] Ibid.   [34] Ibid. 27.   [35] Ibid. 26–7.
[36] Ibid. 27.

discussing dismissively the idea of a just war, Schmitt does allow that resort to war must be against 'a real enemy' and not an imagined one, but he immediately insists that this determination can only be made by the state itself. He says: 'The justification of war does not reside in its being fought for ideals or norms of justice, but in its being fought against a real enemy', but he insists that a state would cease to exist if it allowed the determination of the reality of the enemy to be made independently. If there were room for an independent judgement of 'real enemy' there would be some room for objective moral (or legal) debate and hence for the reintroduction of norms of adjudication that Schmitt is anxious to reject. Such rigid restrictions of the scope of morality as that proposed by Schmitt clearly go well beyond anything that could be countenanced by any normal understanding of the dangers of moralism of scope.

A final point about moralism of scope deserves attention. Although morality can be pertinent to all but the most trivial areas of life, the form that its relevance is sometimes made to take can be destructive or contemptuous of the legitimate intellectual values of that area. There is a form of moralism, as of religiosity, that can insist on what ought to be to the detriment of determining what is. This is parallel to what sometimes happens when religion exceeds its scope, as in the condemnation of Galileo, or in the rejection of the findings of evolutionary science in favour of scriptural literalism. There are elements of moralism in these examples of misplaced religiosity, but perhaps the case is clearest when it comes to arguments about moral issues that have significant political overtones. One such is the debate about AIDS policy where those who oppose the use of condoms on moral grounds, are sometimes led by their moral convictions into absurd empirical claims about the ineffectiveness of condoms as preventers of disease transmission. The issue of effectiveness is not one that inherent moral objections to the use of condoms (as being against the natural law or whatever) can adjudicate, but the moralists in their enthusiasm to discredit political or social endorsement of condoms tend to ride roughshod over the empirical facts. Similarly, in the case of war, an enthusiasm for pursuing a moral agenda, such as establishing democracy in benighted parts of the world, can make one believe that military and intelligence information that runs counter to morally inspired plans must be false. From the other side of the fence, a strong moral commitment to pacifism or simply to reducing resort to war can lead to wishful thinking about the empirical political facts, as happened with the British anti-war movement's failure to appreciate the enormity of the Nazi threat in the 1930s. Of course, outlooks other than morality can also intrude on the legitimacy of military expertise or medical science, but the special role of morality in our lives makes its intrusion unusually seductive.

2

Moralistic Strictures and Political Reality: Further Quandaries

Goodbye Moralitee!

A. P. Herbert, *Lines for a Worthy Person*

In Chapter 1, I concentrated on elucidating the outlook of political realism, introducing the idea of moralism, and beginning an interpretation
of realism in its light. In particular, I explored what I called moralism
of scope which, I argued, makes sense of many versions of the realist
critique of morality by showing that a more plausible target for some
realist criticisms is that form of moralism rather than morality itself. I
also argued that once this adjustment is made, we will be less inclined
to follow realists by attempting to displace morality with appeal to the
national interest, an appeal which, in any case, has its own problems. We
must now take the exploration of moralism and its relation to realism
and to the morality of politics several steps further by examining the
other varieties of moralism mentioned in Chapter 1. I will begin with
the distortion of morality that arises from the giving of an unbalanced
weighting to one set of moral concerns over others that are just as or
more relevant. Call it the moralism of unbalanced focus. An area in
which this type of moralism is common is that of sexual morality. There
is indeed a debate, or many debates, about the nature of sexual morality,
and one of the sharpest points of division concerns that between what
we might call a 'liberal' view of sexual conduct and more traditional
views.[1] The former holds that there is really nothing distinctive about

---

[1] I use the term 'liberal' here because it often used in the philosophical and general
literature on the topic, but I put it in scare quotes because I see no contradiction
in someone's being a liberal in the political sense but having some more traditional
understanding of sexual morality.

the morality of sex; there is no such virtue as chastity to govern sexual relations. For the 'liberal', the basic question is simply one of consent and possibly fairness or justice; rape is wrong because of the lack of consent (and usually violence) involved, but prostitution in non-exploitative circumstances raises no moral issues. Traditional views hold that there is some distinctive good in sexual relations that gives to the area some scope for moral insight broader than the 'liberal' view allows. Of course, there are a wide range of possibilities concerning this scope, and many different views available to traditionalists about the legal implications of a moral stance on the matter. For a variety of reasons, a traditionalist could oppose legal prohibitions on non-exploitative prostitution.

I do not offer an adjudication on these contrasting views here, but the question of moralism of unbalanced focus arises particularly sharply if we grant some mild version of the traditional outlook. (On the 'liberal' outlook, much discourse about sexual morality will involve moralism of scope since the moral terminology is simply not appropriate to the behaviour being denounced.) The point is that it is possible to hold that sexual morality is concerned with a distinctive quality in sexual relations without becoming obsessed with that quality and its significance, and without giving an undue weight to sexual vice amongst the full catalogue of vices. Yet there can be no doubt that there is a tendency amongst traditionalists to do both of these things. For certain clergy and politicians, it would seem that there is no other vice than sexual immorality, and that sexual misdeeds have a peculiar importance that disqualifies perpetrators from high public office or from other sorts of regard or respect. The campaign against President Clinton because of his philandering was partly generated by precisely these attitudes, and, in the United States particularly, the sexual probity of candidates for public office has become an absurdly prominent factor in judging their qualifications. It is true that Clinton's offences at least suggested a more general intemperance and imprudence that might have had wider political significance, though this suggestion hardly rose to the level of proof. In the case of Monica Lewinsky, there were also issues of possible exploitation of an employee, and of deceiving the electorate, but for many who condemned the President these were minor factors. Even traditionalists should concede that sins such as adultery may be relatively unimportant matters when it comes to judging the capacity of a politician to govern or to conduct delicate negotiations with foreign leaders.

One obstacle to conceding as much may be the grip of a partic- ular idea of the connection of the virtues with each other that is embodied in the old philosophical doctrine of the unity of the virtues. There are different ways to interpret this doctrine, but if it means that if you have any virtue then you must have all the virtues (as it seems to mean in a plausible reading of Aristotle and Aquinas) then it flies in the face of all experience of human beings and their complexity as well as making the operation of our moral vocabulary an impossibility. Of course both Aquinas and Aristotle are well aware that it seems as if people can be honest but unchaste or loyal but intemperate with drink, or courageous but unjust. They deny however that these facts are facts about real virtue, rather they describe traits that are not fully virtuous. Aquinas acknowledges that you can have people who, for instance, 'are prompt in doing deeds of liberality, but not of chastity'.[2] (And this more than seven centuries before Bill Clinton!) But he describes such virtue as incomplete or imperfect; it is the 'leaning by nature or habituation towards a type of acting that is in fact good'.[3] By contrast the complete sense of virtue is that in which it concerns 'habits tending towards a good deed well done' and the reference to 'well done' is construed by Aquinas as importing a reference to the virtuous life generally so that the 'strength of soul' involved in courage would not be recommended as virtuous if it were without the moderation or rectitude or discretion found respectively in temperance, justice, and prudence.[4] This is not the place for a full discussion of this doctrine, but whatever the merits of a high theory of virtue that makes it impossible to have a virtue in isolation from one more of the others, it cannot provide a useful attitude to our employment of an everyday vocabulary of the virtues, since we can and must employ such terms as 'courageous', 'honest', 'temperate', 'modest', and the like in many contexts where we have no way of knowing whether the agent in question has the wholehearted commitment to and enjoyment of the plenitude of the virtuous life as required by Aquinas and other supporters of the unity doctrine. In fact, I think there is little to recommend the doctrine even as what I have called high theory, but in the present context it is surely clear that sexual morality, even on the traditional view, is but one area of morality and not always the most relevant to the judicious political treatment of important social questions such as unjust wars, gross social inequality,

---

[2] St Thomas Aquinas, *Summa Theologiae*, 1a.2ae. 65. My quotations are from the Blackfriars edition, gen. ed. Thomas Gilby OP, vol. xxiii, ed. and trans. W. D. Hughes OP, p. 181.

[3] Ibid.   [4] Ibid.

poverty, and access to health care. Where realists warn against bringing private morality to bear upon public questions, it is sometimes this sort of imbalance that they have in mind, even when they make no direct reference to sex. They go wrong, of course, in thinking that our common-sense morality (as Sidgwick called it) is solely concerned with such private matters as sexuality or the having and upbringing of children. When you bring up the topic of morality with teenagers, they often think you must be about to talk about sex (or perhaps drugs or abortion), but this is not a confusion that sophisticated intellectuals should either harbour or encourage.

Sexual morality is not, however, the only arena for moralism of unbalanced focus. Much of the good-hearted support for armed humanitarian intervention seems to me to suffer from this moralistic fault. There is a sort of 'militant humanitarianism', as it has been called, that promotes a very real moral value, namely compassion for those suffering human rights violations, but sometimes to the detriment of other important moral considerations that are also relevant.[5] In particular, some human rights activists who support humanitarian intervention enthusiastically are often blind to the prudential considerations that can militate against it. I have written about this elsewhere, so will be brief here. One of these considerations is that interveners who have the appropriate power often have few of the other attributes that would be necessary for success. They will often have little knowledge of the religious, cultural, and political contexts into which they come with their weapons and bombs, no heart for the long-term repair of the civil order that their intervention commonly further disrupts (even as it rescues), and will quite often have non-humanitarian goals that are inimical to the welfare of the population invaded. The recent invasion of Iraq was not of course humanitarian in its actual motives, but there were many on the 'left' who supported it because it furthered the humanitarian objective of liberating Iraqis from a vicious dictator. Typical of these were the authors in the collection *A Matter of Principle: Humanitarian Arguments for War in Iraq*.[6] The book was published in 2005, but most of the articles were written in 2004. By the later date, some of the authors were

---

[5] The term 'militant humanitarianism' seems to have been coined by Connor Gearty. See his *Can Human Rights Survive?* (Cambridge: Cambridge University Press, 2006), 134.

[6] Thomas Cushman (ed.), *A Matter of Principle: Humanitarian Arguments for War in Iraq* (Berkeley and Los Angeles: University of California Press, 2005).

having second thoughts about their support for humanitarian violence in Iraq, and these second thoughts involved some belated recognition of the imbalance I am discussing.[7] Others, however, were still passionate in their support for the invasion, and this passion was driven by legitimate moral concerns for human rights and revulsion from Saddam's atrocities. The Australian journalist Pamela Bone was particularly eloquent about the moral value of the war, and there is no reason whatever to question her sincerity. Nonetheless, this passion was so lopsided that it induced in her the following astonishing set of claims, apparently referring to the grounds for fighting the war rather than some of its eventual effects: 'Iraq brought together the war against terrorism, Islam versus democracy, national sovereignty versus human rights, secularism versus religious fundamentalism.'[8] I call these claims astonishing because, prior to the invasion, Iraq was not a major player in supporting international terrorism, and it was predominantly a secular state with an interest in containing religious fundamentalism. Thus can moralism of this form militate against realistic assessment.

Such assessment is itself a moral requirement and it needs to moderate our idealist hopes, important as they may be. The dismal consequences of the US-dominated coalition's invasion speak dramatically against these hopes. As I write, Iraq is in a state close to civil war, the invasion having unleashed religious and tribal enmities that had been subdued by the brutal Hussein regime. It has also given opportunities for hitherto non-existent sub-state terrorism in the country as well as the depredations of criminal gangs, and created resentments and rage against the invaders amongst many in the population at large by the arrogant and often racist treatment meted out to Iraqis by troops made edgy and weary by the constant pressure of insurgent war that shows little sign of abating. Abu Ghraib and reported raping and killing by occupying troops are only the tip of the iceberg of this aspect of the disaster. In reply, two things may be said. One is that it is easy to be wise after the event, and the other is that Iraq is a bad case to take. The former would be a reasonable response if it were not for the fact that many predicted something resembling this sort of outcome. I was in Atlanta, Georgia, a few days after the invasion began,

---

[7] Mitchell Cohen's contribution to the debate shows such qualms, and is notably less prone to moralism of unbalanced focus than a number of the other authors. See Cohen, 'In the Murk of It: Iraq Reconsidered', in Cushman (ed.), *A Matter of Principle*, 76–92.

[8] Pamela Bone, 'They Don't Know One Little Thing', in Cushman (ed.), *A Matter of Principle*, 302.

and the *Atlanta Journal-Constitution* (not a notably radical organ) had a front-page story accurately forecasting many of the dangers that would face the post-war occupiers.[9] It is now known that many senior military figures were sceptical about the prospects of success in an operation of the kind proposed by President Bush and Mr Rumsfeld.[10] The second response is not available to those militant humanitarians who supported the invasion, but it is true that there was a much better case for military action in, for instance, Rwanda. My argument is not that all humanitarian military intervention must be flawed, but that the enthusiasm for this sort of solution to human rights abuses often exhibits the moralism of unbalanced focus and thereby ignores or downplays the horrors that even well-motivated war usually involves. In just war terminology, the militant humanitarians focus obsessively upon the just cause, and ignore the weighty moral considerations encapsulated in the conditions of prospect of success, last resort, and proportionality. Moreover, they often have too narrow a focus upon what success should consist in. It is indeed a good thing that the murderous tyrant Saddam is gone, and that he has no further opportunity to kill and despoil on the massive scale that he did. The evil acts of his regime must be acknowledged, and they legitimately had weight in thinking about an international response to Iraq. But the destabilizing of the Middle East, the greatly increased impetus to terrorism, the benefits to the power of Iran, and the descent of Iraq into civic chaos are colossal prices to pay. Indeed, according to one reputable estimate, published in 2006, there has been an increase of 655,000 Iraqi deaths directly attributable to the invasion of 2003 and its aftermath.[11] In addition, there has been a massive exodus of Iraqi people to other countries, though recently some refugees have returned. The militant humanitarians couldn't have forecast exactly these outcomes, but the influence of moralism on their thinking blinded too many of

[9] Mark Davis, 'Tough Days Ahead for Troops: As Campaign Moves from Desert, Deadly Urban Warfare Expected', *Atlanta Journal-Constitution* (24 Mar. 2003).

[10] See e.g. the discussion in Marybeth P. Ulrich and Martin L. Cook, 'US Civil Military Relations since 9/11: Issues in Ethics and Policy Development', *Journal of Military Ethics*, 5/3 (2006), esp. 167–70.

[11] Gilbert Burnham, Riyadh Lafta, Shannon Doocy, and Les Roberts, 'Morality after the 2003 Invasion of Iraq: A Cross-Sectional Cluster Sample Survey', *The Lancet* (21 Oct. 2006). Supporters of the war have been quick to challenge these figures, but the methodology behind the findings and the integrity of the investigators were endorsed shortly after the controversy surrounding their publication by a group of twenty-seven distinguished medical scientists in an article in the Melbourne *Age* (21 Oct. 2006), 'The Iraq deaths study was valid and correct', Insight, 9.

them to the probability of outcomes of this kind. These outcomes, of course, precisely embody the sort of considerations that realists typically adduce in order to counterbalance the concern with moral principles and high moral values.

Another thing that is sometimes referred to as moralism, and would come under the category of unbalanced focus, is the insistence on cold, punitive moral attitudes to the exclusion of warmer moral concerns such as compassion, forgiveness, and mercy. This unbalance is one of the themes of Hawthorn's *The Scarlet Letter,* but it can have wider implications than the domestic setting there involved.[12] Many of these unbalanced punitive attitudes lie behind some excesses of law and order campaigns, such as 'three strikes, you're out' laws and other pressures aimed at removing room for judicial discretion in punishment. In fairness, it should be added that the imbalance can sometimes result from an emphasis on the softer virtues to the exclusion of the sterner. Critics of 'truth and reconciliation' tribunals and procedures argue that there is precisely this lack of balance in them, because the needs of justice are neglected, submerged, or downgraded by a distorting focus on reconciliation.[13] There will indeed often be room for nuanced judgement and genuine disagreement about where the correct balance between different moral values should lie, so differences on such matters as punishment or attitudes towards offenders cannot always be treated as involving moralism. But where legitimate contrasting moral concerns are simply ignored or persistently treated as irrelevant or insignificant, it is plausible to see this form of moralism as a factor.

MORALISM OF IMPOSITION OR INTERFERENCE

Like moralism of scope, this concerns inappropriate resort to morality, but this sort of moralism does not involve invalid moral judgements per se. Rather, its error is to insist that what may well be valid moral judgements on their subject matter be imposed inappropriately on other

[12] For a good discussion of the moralism involved (and condemned) in the story of Hawthorn's *The Scarlet Letter,* see Craig Taylor, 'Moralism and Morally Accountable Beings', in Coady (ed.), *What's Wrong with Moralism?*

[13] David A. Crocker, 'Retribution and Reconciliation', *Philosophy and Public Policy Quarterly,* 20 (Winter/Spring 2000), 1–6; repr. in Verna V. Gehring and William A. Galston (eds.), *Philosophical Dimensions of Public Policy,* Policy Studies Review Annual, 13 (New Brunswick, NJ and London: Transaction, 2002), 211–19.

people. This is related to the liberal outlook on non-interference and recent debates about the neutrality of the State. But the problems raised by the idea of imposition cut much deeper than the role of the State, since there is a set of issues about what the virtue of tolerance requires that views those requirements as social and moral as well as political. This has begun to receive serious philosophical attention only in recent years. Important features needing scrutiny are: (1) the degree of certainty that can attach to one's moral judgements and the relation of this to responses to the moral judgements of others; (2) the moral importance of respecting other people's moral judgements as a tribute to their dignity as moral agents, and the limits to this; (3) the degree to which making moral judgements about the behaviour of others has any significance beyond the aim of improving one's own character and behaviour (and protecting oneself and others from their harm-causing); (4) the extent to which certain expressions of moral judgement betray faulty estimates of one's own self-importance and role in the lives of others, and a connected incapacity for moral self-criticism; (5) the degree to which acting on moral judgements about the behaviour of people from other cultures shows a culpable disrespect for their culture. A full discussion of moralism of imposition will, of course, have to scrutinize more carefully the idea of 'imposition' itself since its employment in popular and theoretical contexts is riddled with confusions.[14] One of the major complications here is that engendered by the stance of moral relativism in its various forms. One of the least attractive but highly influential forms is that of simple cultural relativism (hereafter SCR) which makes it seem as though the only route to tolerance is by denial of the validity of any cross-cultural or supra-cultural moral judgements. In fact, support for tolerance, in any of its five aspects mentioned above, is unlikely to come from imprisoning moral validity within cultures since most cultures in varying degrees have embodied deeply intolerant norms, and advocacy of tolerance requires resort to subtle and complex reasoning

---

[14] For recent work on tolerance and its complexities, see e. g. Julia Driver, 'Hyperactive Ethics', *Philosophical Quarterly*, 44/174 (1994), 9–25; David Heyd, *Toleration: An Elusive Virtue* (Princeton: Princeton University Press, 1996), and Michael Walzer, *On Toleration* (New Haven: Yale University Press, 1997). For the most influential modern statement on State tolerance of divergent 'conceptions of the good' see John Rawls, *Political Liberalism* (New York: Columbia University Press, 1993), and for a classical statement of early liberal defences of political tolerance, see John Locke, *Letters On Toleration* (Byculla: Education Society's Press, 1867).

and insight that goes beyond parochial standards. Nor is it persuasive to claim that relativism somehow leads to tolerance, even if it does not logically support it, since the idea that my moral values have no need to answer to independent criteria of reason may simply unleash my will to power, a point that the late, unlamented Benito Mussolini saw clearly.[15] Robustly tolerant practices spring from a vigorous human virtue that can be recommended to all people, not from some supposed incapacity to think beyond the boundaries of one's own social conditioning.

In addition to this, SCR is prone to many intellectual difficulties, as numerous philosophical commentators have observed. It is, I believe, ill-supported by the principal arguments adduced on its behalf—notably the arguments from divergence and from the need for a framework—but I have no space to show that now (and it has, in any case, been argued decisively by others). SCR also involves a simplistic treatment of cultures as wholly unified entities, ignoring the diversity of moral outlooks within even the simplest cultures, and makes the possibility of moral advance and reform incoherent. In its anxiety to avoid the condemnation of other culture's values, it also makes it impossible to praise or learn from them. More sophisticated versions of relativism have been developed in response to these difficulties, and they allow that some moral beliefs are better than others, that reason has a place in developing moral views, and that there are ways of legitimately criticizing at least some moral views of other cultures in a fashion that is not parochial.[16] But such sophistication makes cultural relativism and other forms of relativism irrelevant to the broad view of imposition that we are considering and that has influenced many realists. These more elaborate theories offer no support to such dramatic views as Morgenthau's, for instance, who triumphantly quotes Edmund Burke as saying: 'Nothing universal can

---

[15] Mussolini's exact words are worth quoting in full: 'Everything that I have said and done in these last years is relativism by intuition. From the fact that all ideologies are of equal value, that all ideologies are mere fictions, the relativist infers that everybody has the right to create for himself his own ideology and to attempt to enforce it with all the energy of which he is capable. If relativism signifies contempt for fixed categories and men who claim to be the bearers of an objective, immortal truth, then there is nothing more relativistic than fascism.' Quoted in Henry Veatch, 'A Critique of Benedict', in Julius R. Weinberg and Keith Yandell (eds.), *Problems in Philosophical Inquiry* (New York: Holt, Rinehard and Winston Inc., 1971), 27.

[16] Simon Blackburn, 'Relativism', in Hugh LaFollette (ed.), *The Blackwell Guide to Ethical Theory* (Malden, Mass.: Blackwell, 2001).

be rationally affirmed on any moral or any political subject.'[17] If this is itself, as it seems, an affirmation on a moral or political subject then its lack of rationality hardly commends it to anyone, least of all realists who tend to put a premium on rationality. In particular, it undermines the realist obsession with the rationality of the concern for the national interest.[18]

Hence I will take it that imposition is a narrower notion that involves some degree of force, coercion, or disrespect for autonomy, though the operation of that force, coercion or disrespect may be subtle. It is thus itself to be condemned where appropriate on moral grounds, as is the very closely related phenomenon known as 'judgementalism'. There need however be no imposition involved in forming the judgement that some other person or group's behaviour is immoral, nor need there be in telling them that it is. This is especially true if the verdict is requested, for it is surely absurd to see ordinary examples of moral advice as impositions. Even where advice is not sought and is unwelcome, the giving of it need not be impositional; there is a world of difference between writing a private letter of protest at another's bad behaviour and sending in the marines. Of course, speech acts, including those with moral content, can be improperly coercive or disrespectful, but they are not necessarily so—it all depends on the way they are done. We need to be alert both to the right and wrong ways of expressing moral criticism and admonishment, something of which good parents are particularly aware. It is even possible that reasoning itself be used as an illegitimate weapon to overpower another's autonomous thinking. Someone with superior intellectual powers can use those powers with insufficient respect for

---

[17] Quoted by Michael Joseph Smith, in *Realist Thought from Weber to Kissinger* (Baton Rouge: Louisiana State University Press, 1986), 164.

[18] Smith correctly points out that the Burke dictum would count equally against Morgenthau's own advocacy of the universal importance of the pursuit of the national interest. Other advocates of realism also seek the support of relativism. E. H. Carr, for instance, confidently proclaims the relativity of all thought, but like many before and since tends to confuse the questions of origin and validation. Carr says that the ethical standards of 'utopians' have been shown by realists not to be the 'expression of absolute and a priori principles' but 'historically conditioned, being both products of circumstances and interests and weapons framed for the further-ance of interests' (Carr, *The Twenty Year Crisis*, 68). Yet there is no barrier to a belief's being unconditionally true that it was produced in specific historical circum-stances and promoted certain interests. The belief that certain fruits are poisonous arose from unfortunate experiences with eating them and is propagated to pre-vent their causing harm, but may be categorically true and known to be so, for all that.

the insights, experience, and grounded understanding of another who is less skilled in the arts of reasoning. Intellectuals are understandably reluctant to admit such a possibility, but bullying by intellectual power is as real as bullying by physical strength. Such bullying can occur in the use of moral as well as other reasoning. Nonetheless, it is a distortion of something genuine, and moral advice, persuasion, or criticism need not be an exercise of illicit power. The idea that any communication of a moral judgement or moral reasoning to another party, especially where the judgement or conclusion is adverse, must be impositional, seems dependent on some version of simple cultural relativism.

MORALISM OF ABSTRACTION

In both common discourse, and, increasingly, in academic writings, people are often criticized for operating morally at a level too abstract, or lofty, to achieve realistic engagement with the world of action. Sometimes the objection to the lofty principles or ideals is that they are too universal for the diversity of the world and of agents, sometimes it is that they are too rationalistic for the emotional, intuitive, concretely responsive agents that we are, sometimes that they are too simplistic in their formulation, or sometimes that they are too incapable of realization, but the general drift is that the abstract apparatus of morality (or sometimes, moral theory) essentially cannot satisfactorily fit the world it is supposedly made for. Machiavelli's advice to the Prince to 'learn how not to be good' and to shun various virtues (in certain contexts) because they will lead to ruin is based partly upon a profound challenge to certain underlying assumptions inherent in most moral outlooks, and partly upon a confusion of morality with simplistic moralistic distortions of it of the kind here considered. The latter can be seen in some of Machiavelli's complaints about the inappropriateness of virtues like generosity in a Prince. He claims that the generous prince lavishes gifts and bounty thereby emptying his coffers and encouraging insurrection. But the lesson to be drawn is not that virtue is inappropriate for a Prince, or even that this virtue has no place, but that the proper exercise of virtue is highly sensitive to circumstance. Generosity will display different features in different contexts. Instead of requiring miserliness, as Machiavelli suggests, what is appropriate to the Prince is a proper frugality (without which generosity makes little sense). The Machiavelli criticism also raises the important question of roles. Much realist criticism of the employment of morality emphasizes the distinctive tasks of rulers or politicians, and the ways in which the sphere of operations in which they are involved differs so much from that of other roles. The moralizing that realists object to is precisely that which covers reality with an undifferentiated moral blanket, instead of cutting the moral cloth to fit the different roles that agents play. So Dean Acheson writes:

As one probes further into the moral aspects of relations between states, additional causes for treading warily appear. A little reflection will convince us that the same conduct is not moral under all circumstances. Its moral propriety seems to depend, certainly in many cases, upon the relationship of those concerned with the conduct. For instance, parents have the moral right, indeed duty, to instil moral and religious ideas in their children and punish error. Ministers, priests, rabbis, and mullahs have much the same duties to their flocks, including that of correcting heresy, when they can make up their minds what it is. But these same acts on the part of public officials in the United States would be both immoral and a denial of the fundamental rights of the citizen.[19]

Acheson is clearly right to worry about the blurring of lines between preacher and politician, indeed his warning looks astonishingly prescient since it was issued more than forty years before the triumph of the religious right in the USA resulted in the election of George W. Bush. Not only does President Bush often sound more like a fundamentalist Christian preacher than the president of a multicultural country that insists upon the separation of church and state, but his appeals to morality are frequently offered at a level of rhetorical abstraction that notably fails to mesh with the specific realities they purport to address. Perhaps the most striking example of this is the President's persistent framing of political issues, especially international issues, in terms of a simple conflict between good and evil, good being principally located in the United States (or sometimes, broader Western alliances) and evil in the enemy or opponents. Peter Singer has noted that Bush referred to evil in 319 speeches between his inauguration and the middle of 2003, approximately 30 per cent of all the speeches he gave in that period. As Singer also notes, the

---

[19] Dean Acheson, 'Morality, Moralism and Diplomacy', *Yale Review*, 47/4 (June 1958), 488.

vast majority of the President's uses of the word 'evil' is in the noun form rather than adjectival (914 against 182) and in only a handful of cases is the adjectival form used to describe human acts or deeds.[20] Considering that many Presidential speeches are on mundane matters, that is a remarkable figure and, given subsequent international conflicts, the ratio is unlikely to have declined since 2003. The President's mind is clearly dominated by a picture of Good and Evil as metaphysical entities with their own power to determine outcomes through representative human agencies. Many have noted the influence of an Apocalyptic strain of fundamentalist Christianity upon the President and this goes some way to account for his Manichaean addiction to the great abstractions of Good and Evil in place of more nuanced accounts of the rights and wrongs of political realities. In so far as Dean Acheson's realism is warning against the moralism of abstraction implicit in a simplified conflation of faith commitments and complex political realities, his comments are salutary, indeed almost prophetically so!

Nonetheless, Acheson's remarks contain the seeds of some confusion. He seems on the verge of making too strong a dichotomy between public and private and the morality suitable to each. The suggestion is that private morality is all very well in its place, but its dictates and inhibitions are quite out of place in politics. Sometimes, the thesis is the more restrictive one that they are out of place in foreign affairs. The proper attention to roles required, however, is more sensitive to moral realities than any crude and ambiguous contrast of public and private. This contrast is useful for some purposes, but in the present context it is too artificial and blunt for the issues that need to be confronted. The usual points about how the role of statesman makes a difference to what one is obliged and entitled to do, can also be made about such roles as parent or friend which are clearly on the private side of the divide, or about the role of teacher which straddles the distinction. Of course, the arguments will point to different obligations and entitlements in the different cases. Here I am merely interested in structural similarities in the argument for roles in both the private and public domains. There is an obvious truth in the idea that roles make a moral difference, even if Acheson's contrasts can point in directions

---

[20] Peter Singer, *The President of Good and Evil: The Ethics of George W. Bush* (Melbourne: Text Publishing, 2004), 2.

that are too simplistic. But that truth is not something that somehow negates broad moral assessments since we need an overarching moral rationale for the existence of roles and the special permissions and duties that they involve. This is obviously true of conventional or 'socially constructed' roles but it is also true in more complex ways of relatively natural roles, like mother or friend. If the imperatives and permissions associated with roles were not under moral control, then those related to embezzler and burglar would have the same status as those of doctor and lawyer. By contrast with crime, medicine and the place it occupies in our lives is morally supported by the significance of healing, and the surgeon's entitlements to cut people up and her duty to maintain the confidentiality of patients' personal details arise from that value (as well as from complex matters of consent). Similar considerations clearly apply to the law and policing. The detailed operation of role moralities can be challenged by criticizing the connection of the duties and permissions with the broader moral purposes of the role (as some lawyer privileges might be rejected as failing to serve justice or the rights of the accused) and they may be overruled by other moral considerations, as when confidentiality is outweighed by the need to prevent a disaster. Acheson is right to point to role differentiation, and to emphasize the way religious instruction and exhortation should be beyond the remit of public officials. Indeed, this is a lesson that the United States political leadership needs to relearn. But he is wrong to imply (as he seems to) that there is no room for general moral critique of the operation of roles, especially political roles. Some lofty moral criticism (and some abstract moral theorizing) may fail to take full account of the differentiation and its significance, but this cannot imply that the norms that operate in a role (including the role of international diplomat or foreign secretary) are immune to criticism, or indeed support, that draws its resources from fully informed general moral perspectives or, for that matter, from suitably nuanced moral theory.

ABSOLUTIST MORALISM

This is closely related to the moralism of abstraction, and might have been treated under that head, but it has certain distinctive features that license separate discussion. As we saw earlier, the charge of 'moral absolutism' is brought by Schlesinger against his targets who don't understand the 'necessary amorality' of much of foreign affairs, and it is a charge echoed by other realists. The term 'absolutism' needs to be handled carefully. Where it is opposed to 'relativism' then anyone who rejects various forms of moral relativism will be an absolutist, but this is not usually what people like Schlesinger mean by the term, and, if they do, then they are likely to inherit some of the problems discussed earlier in connection with cultural relativism. It is better to oppose 'relativism' to 'objectivism' and reserve 'absolutism' for the view that some moral prohibitions hold come what may. We can then see the realist objection to absolutism as an objection to a certain sort of moral inflexibility. Now it may be that there are some moral prohibitions that are absolute, but it is important to note that the most plausible version of this outlook holds that there are very few of them.[21] So, it may be that the intentional killing of the innocent or even the infliction of torture are absolutely wrong, in this sense, while it remains that many other serious prohibitions, such as those against lying, promise-breaking, and violations of confidentiality are open to exception. With these qualifications, the charge of moralism in this form amounts to an objection to inflexibility or rigorism in the application of moral categories and it is akin to the moralism of abstraction discussed earlier. It is also linked in the realist outlook with the idea of fanaticism, an obsessive concentration on some moral value or judgement to the detriment of a sense of balance in estimating the place of that value or judgement in a wider scheme of things or in particular contexts. One of the most interesting aspects of this in both interpersonal and international settings, is the phenomenon of demonization. This is the casting of some individual or group in the role of a purely malevolent agent. It is sometimes objected to this that there can be no such figures because there is no such thing as evil. This is not an objection I shall press since I think that there certainly is evil in the world and that it is sometimes exhibited in human action, though probably less commonly than often supposed. My complaint about demonization is different. I think demonization has three morally bad effects. First, it tends to miss the mark thereby subjecting largely innocent, innocuous, or mildly errant groups or individuals to unwarranted contempt or persecution. This is clearly something that some politicians in my country, and

---

[21] See e. g. John Finnis, *Moral Absolutes: Tradition, Revision and Truth* (Washington DC: Catholic University of America Press, 1991).

perhaps elsewhere, have recently done disgracefully to refugees. The tendency is also at work in the treatment of Islamic communities. Second, demonization reduces the demonized to a malevolent force with no other motivation than the promotion of pure evil. Vile leaders like Hitler and Stalin come close to fitting this caricature, but even they had more intelligible and human motives for some of their deeds and misdeeds than this picture suggests. Realists are right to worry that the moral categorization can displace attention from other human and empirical realities that are relevant to action. It seems plausible that the demonization of Saddam Hussein contributed significantly to the gross Western misjudgements about his weapons of mass destruction. Horrible as Saddam was, he should have been credited with human instincts of self-preservation and with various other mundane motives (such as resentment and need to preserve 'face') that contributed to his often-ambiguous behaviour in response to outside pressure. Third, demonization both arises from and contributes to what might be called lopsided moralism. Not only does demonizing localize and focus evil in a particular person, group, or region, it then blurs the features and workings of evil elsewhere, most notably close to home. This makes for a deficient understanding not only of the enemy but, even more importantly, of oneself. The talk of 'bad guys' is inevitably accompanied by the talk of 'good guys' and this childish simplicity leads to the profound absurdity of President Bush's belief that 'they hate us because we're so good'.

Another manifestation of undue rigorism is the reluctance to face the necessity for adapting moral rules to the exigencies of compromise, the difficulties of extrication from moral messes of one's making (or those one has inherited), and the pitfalls of moral isolation. These are three categories of situation that I have explored elsewhere, but which are frequently encountered in political contexts.

Here I will briefly address only the relevance of compromise.[22] Compromise is ever-present in politics and can be felt as a threat, a challenge, or an opportunity, and sometimes all three. Its pervasiveness

---

[22] For further discussion of compromise, and detailed discussion of the problems of extrication and moral isolation see C. A. J. Coady, 'Messy Morality and the Art of the Possible', *Proceedings of the Aristotelian Society*, suppl. 64 (1990), esp 267–79. The issue of extrication also addressed at length in Coady, 'Escaping from the Bomb', in Henry Shue (ed.), *Nuclear Deterrence and Moral Restraint* (New York: Cambridge University Press, 1989), 193–216.

arises from the fact that politics is inevitably both collaborative and adversarial (or at least conflictual). It can genuinely be a threat when the need to strike a bargain overwhelms commitment to core values to such a degree that the agent's integrity is destroyed. Then we speak of that individual as compromised. Yet although compromise often has a hint of moral danger to it, someone who can seldom or never adjust their policies, projects, or hopes to the desires, interests, and contrary plans of those they must work with suffers from a defect of character. To turn everything you value into a matter of basic principle is not to show moral strength but moralistic inflexibility. Even with very important moral commitments, an agent may in context show more moral wisdom in postponing legal measures to implement them, than in damaging their cause by stubbornly advocating measures that have no realistic prospect of success. Someone who is totally opposed to abortion may do better to support measures that legalize early abortions but not late-term ones or someone opposed to the death penalty may further their project better by instituting or supporting measures drastically to restrict its use. There is no rubric for deciding what are the limits of compromise, when it is an exercise of practical wisdom and when it is a betrayal of deep principle, since the detailed circumstances and the nature of the principle need to be judiciously appreciated *in situ*. Nonetheless, it needs to be understood that compromise is not only often a practical necessity in politics, but also that it *can* be dictated by a respect for the conscientiously held values and the dignity of those who disagree with you. This is especially so when issues are morally complex and genuinely contentious.

MORALISM OF DELUDED POWER

This is less a distorted form of moral judgement or understanding, than a distorted belief in the power of moral utterances and moral stands, often accompanied by a sense of self-righteousness. Moralism of this sort is the mistaken, or at least overconfident, belief that appeals to moral standards, ideals, and principles will have by themselves powerful effects in altering behaviour. Realists oppose this belief and phenomena associated with it because they think that it ignores the realities of international behaviour, and in particular the realities of power and self-interest. It can also far too often provide a camouflage, wittingly or unwittingly, for the promotion of interests that have little to do with morality. This can be seen vividly in the realist George Kennan's denunciations of the politics of moral rhetoric. The following is taken from Kennan's 'Morality and Foreign Policy' (1985) in which he calls for 'the avoidance of what might be called the histrionics of moralism at the expense of its substance'. He continues:

By that is meant the projection of attitudes, poses and rhetoric that cause us to appear noble and altruistic in the mirror of our own vanity but lack substance when related to the realities of international life. It is a sad feature of the human predicament, in personal as in public life, that whenever one has the agreeable sensation of being impressively moral, one probably is not.[23]

This catches both the delusional belief in the efficacy of mere high-sounding words, and the self-deceptive element so often characteristic of moralism. Again, this realist emphasis is instructive and might usefully be brought to the attention of many of the world's leaders today when overblown moral (and sometimes religious) rhetoric is so prominent. But Kennan is not denouncing sober moral talk or sensible moral judgement on world affairs, as is clear from his final point that the agreeable sensation of being moral is a bad indicator of the presence of true morality. His strictures are against a form of moralism not morality.

Kennan's accurate account of this form of the vice is unfortunately conjoined with a version of simple cultural relativism that itself owes something to the vice. In the paper from which his comments were quoted, he casts a rather jaundiced eye upon the role played by the discourse of human rights in foreign policy. Discussing various American interventions in the affairs of other nations undertaken on behalf of defending human rights or other serious moral concerns, Kennan raises some telling points about the way in which moral indignation or denunciation can hinder one's grasp of intractable realities. His warnings were given more than twenty years ago, but remain sadly pertinent today. But too often he pins this defect to the idea that moral judgements can only be validated from the partial viewpoint of a particular political culture. So he says:

When we talk about the application of moral standards to foreign policy, therefore, we are not talking about compliance with some generally accepted

---

[23] George F. Kennan, 'Morality and Foreign Policy', originally in *Foreign Affairs*, 64/2 (Winter 1985/6), 205–18, and reprinted as an appendix in Kenneth M. Jensen and Elizabeth P. Faulkner (eds.), *Morality and Foreign Policy* (Washington DC: United States Institute of Peace, 1991), 69. Page references are to the reprinted version.

international code of behaviour. If the policies and actions of the US government are to be made to conform to moral standards, those standards are going to have to be America's own, founded on traditional American principles of justice and propriety. . . . When others fail to conform to those principles [we cannot] . . . assume that our moral standards are theirs as well . . . [24]

Here there are two egregious errors, the first perhaps slightly more forgivable than the second. The first simply ignores the very widespread international acceptance of moral standards of behaviour that applied even in 1985. Consider, for example, the concept of an 'atrocity' broadly employed and mutually understood by all sides in many discussions of war and rebellion (though often misused for propaganda purposes) and the significant degree of acceptance of the UN Charter across very divergent cultures. Kennan's error here may be partly excusable when one considers the polemics of the Cold War then at one of its heights, and the political rhetoric of many dictatorships that invoked 'Asian values' and other convenient catch-cries to fend off criticism from within and without of their corrupt and damaging practices. The widespread achievements subsequently of international humanitarian law and human rights activism plus the collapse, increasing vulnerability, or partial reform of the regimes who treated all criticism of their behaviour as 'Western imposition' have made Kennan's view even more indefensible than it was at the time. His second error is the idea that serious moral criticism of the behaviour of nations by Americans must rest on premises internal to the American tradition. The implicit arrogance of this idea echoes the sort of arrogance that Kennan is usually so good at exposing. Criticism of US national policy by Americans need not be restricted by customary American traditions of 'justice and propriety' since they can be built on more fundamental insights which are widely shared across cultures. Indeed, the best American traditions are informed by these wider insights though they have also contributed to them, and many American traditions about 'justice and propriety' that are peculiar to the United States are ambiguous and sometimes debased, witness the addiction to capital punishment (including, in principle if seldom in practice, that of minors) and the obsession with the propriety of widespread access to lethal weapons.[25]

[24] Ibid. 63.
[25] There is another form of moralism that I do not treat here because it has less direct bearing upon political morality. This is a moralism of inappropriate explicitness, a form of moralism that is often invoked as a criticism in connection with literature. The idea

There is an element of morality that is often a specific target of realist complaints but that I have not treated explicitly so far. This is reliance upon ideals. Here, as elsewhere, realists tend to shoot pretty indiscriminately, and from the hip, seldom pausing to distinguish ideals from other moral categories. In this, they are seduced perhaps by the idea that all morality is somehow idealistic, especially in the context of power politics. But ideals form only a part of morality, and a puzzling and philosophically ill-explored part at that. In the next chapter, I shall attempt to remedy that defect and elaborate more fully on the nature of ideals and their relevance to morality and to politics. It is enough to note here that realist uneasiness with ideals is probably related to two features of ideals. One is that ideals appear to be, in some sense, unrealizable and hence fall victim to the defects involved in moralism of scope and perhaps of abstraction. How can something that cannot be achieved be relevant to a morality of politics? Second, ideals can appear to belong to a part of morality that is more easily viewed with a relativist eye. Your ideal of asceticism need not be mine, for I may live the life of a (moderate) *bon vivant*, but we are neither of us immoral in our divergent attitudes. Or so it may seem. Seeming thus, invocation of ideals may readily fall victim to moralism of imposition. Clearly, more needs to be done with this topic, and I will attend to it in Chapter 3.

In conclusion, I hope to have shown that, properly understood, the doctrine of realism has something to teach about the role of morality in international affairs. Broadly that lesson is: beware of moralism. It is a salutary lesson, not of course restricted to foreign relations, but particularly significant there, because the damage that can be done is so great. What specific guidance will be drawn from such a warning will depend upon the particular circumstances involved. I have tried to show that some of the typical realist claims about what are actually moralistic policies and in what their moralism consists are highly debatable. Realist prescriptions for avoiding moralism are sometimes useful, sometimes not. It is folly, and sadly a folly to which realists are prone to succumb, to see the only alternative to moralism as some form of national egoism. We might compare this with a parallel reaction

is that an author shows a certain defect in moral and aesthetic sensitivity in being too overt about the moral lessons to be drawn from his or her work. Hence, such an author is likely to be accused of moralism or moralizing for succumbing to this fault. For more discussion of this see, C. A. J. Coady, 'The Moral Reality in Realism', *Journal of Applied Philosophy*, 22/2 (2005), 131–2.

to moralism at the personal level. It would be absurd to think that a retreat into relentless selfishness was the only feasible response to the haughty unreality of Pecksniff's smug assessments in Dickens's *Martin Chuzzlewit* or the cruel and arrogant judgementalism of the Puritan townsfolk in Hawthorn's *The Scarlet Letter*.[26] Such moralizing stands exposed and condemned by morality itself, not by mere self-interest. Similarly, a recognition of the dangers of moralism in the international (or national) arena is itself morally driven and needs the response of a healthy, prudent moral understanding. It will of course need to take account of the realities of international interactions, including those generated by power relations and the duties of group representation. But these do not negate the moral categories underlying any form of moral response. A proper concern for national well-being will have a place in such a response, but only one place amongst others. The right replacement for moralism is not national self-interest, but a suitably nuanced and attentive international morality.[27]

---

[26] See Robert Fullinwider's 'On Moralism', in Coady (ed.), *What's Wrong with Moralism?*, for an analysis of Pecksniff's moralism and Craig Taylor's 'Moralism and Morally Accountable Beings' in the same collection for an account of the moralism that destroys Hester in the Hawthorn novel.

[27] A full debate about the appropriate contours of such a morality would have to advert to current controversies about the status of what are called 'cosmopolitan' moralities and their rivals, especially with respect to the concept of justice. There is burgeoning literature on this topic. Just a few notable books are: John Rawls, *The Law of Peoples* (Cambridge, Mass.: Harvard University Press, 1999); Thomas Pogge, *World Poverty and Human Rights* (Cambridge: Polity Press, 2002); Henry Shue, *Basic Rights: Subsistence, Affluence and US Foreign Policy*, 2nd edn. (Princeton: Princeton University Press, 1996); Peter Singer, *One World: The Ethics of Globalization* (New Haven: Yale University Press, 2002); David Miller, *On Nationality* (Oxford: Oxford University Press, 1995); Darrel Moellendorf, *Cosmopolitan Justice* (Oxford: Westview Press, 2002); Martha Nussbaum, *Frontiers of Justice: Disability, Nationality, Species Membership* (Cambridge, Mass.: Belknap Press, 2005).

3

Concerning Ideals

> Howls the sublime, and softly sleeps the calm Ideal, in the whispering chambers of Imagination.
>
> Charles Dickens, *Martin Chuzzlewit*

Ideals have had something of a bad press amongst intellectuals in the last third of the twentieth century. Often enough, they have been denounced as dangerous and delusional, especially though not exclusively by the realist thinkers we discussed earlier. On the other hand, many theorists ignore them altogether, partly, perhaps, because of the belief that they have been shown to be dangerous and delusional and hence require no more attention, but also because the emphasis of philosophical inquiry has been concentrated elsewhere. Amongst moral philosophers, the neglect for most of the twentieth century was very striking especially when compared to the amount of ink spilled, or computer keys attacked, on such topics as virtue, utility, duty, or obligation. Yet exploration of the nature, structure, and role of ideals has a clear relevance to practical life and thinking, and, as I shall argue, it is implausible to hold that the function of ideals in our lives must be wholly malign or trivial. Ideals are also relevant to theoretical discussion in moral and political philosophy, as indicated by the recent outbreak of debate about the meaning and implications of the ideal of equality. Beyond theory, ideals have long been held to be significant in the practice of politics, or at least in statecraft, and a recognition of the importance of ideals in politics is a good part of what lies behind the widespread complaints that contemporary democratic politicians are mere 'pragmatists'. Rejection of ideals cannot rest with mere dismissal; it needs to make a case. In what follows, I shall examine and criticize the case that could be made.

Some of the discomfort felt about ideals arises from their apparent conflict with certain elements in our moral thinking: for one thing, the fact that morality must be attentive to possibility and feasibility. If ideals have some significance in the moral life then this significance is likely to be in tension with the demands of practicality, feasibility, and even possibility, for by its nature the ideal stands in opposition to the real. Of course, this opposition needs unpacking, and it is not always what it seems. Another source of disquiet is the fear that ideals are all too realizable, or nearly so, and that this is often a bad thing. This is the primary burden of the realist critique of ideals mentioned towards the end of Chapter 2.

The ambiguity in our attitude to ideals emerges from deep in the earth of our intellectual history. Ever since Plato, the thought that there is something perfect and other which contrasts with the imperfect, familiar world of experience, and connection with which will provide sense, order, and guidance to our lives has been both seductive and repellent. Plato's (or Socrates') realm of Forms seemed to promise a semantic, epistemic, moral, and even political wholeness that could take us out of the Cave, and it is significant that the very word 'ideal' derives in part from the Platonic concern for the realm of forms or ideas. In the contemporary world, ideals seem to have suffered some reflected distaste from the emphatic rejection of political utopias that is such a feature of our reactions to the devastating ugliness of the pursuit of totalitarian ideals in the twentieth century. Yet ideals, whether explicitly acknowledged or not, continue to exercise a power in our thinking and acting that needs explanation. Though much else was in play, the 2003 invasion of Iraq illustrates this power quite clearly in the appeals on one side of the debate to the ideal of democratic government and on the other to the ideal of peace. Any explanation of the moral and political significance of ideals will have to locate it in a landscape that is replete with obligations, duties, commitments, permissions, and roles.

A beginning can be made in charting the place of ideals by exploring some distinctions between ideals and goals. Ideals are like goals, in that they orient our strivings, desires, and practical reasonings, but they are unlike ordinary goals in at least four ways. (Much of what follows in this paragraph is applicable, *mutatis mutandis*, to the distinction between ideals and values.) First, they are more comprehensive and general than most goals. An ideal of physical fitness is different in this way from the goal of getting a good night's sleep (though the two may be related). Second, there is a necessary element of what I shall call 'esteem' in an ideal that need not be present in a goal. An ideal is estimable for those who pursue or acknowledge it in that they must rank it highly as a good. They need not view it as endowed with moral significance, at least on a common and perhaps rather narrow understanding of morality, since there are, for instance, aesthetic and possibly religious ideals that many would hesitate to describe as moral. Goals on the other hand need not be estimable in this way. They will of course be values, in the sense of being objects of desire and quest, but they need not be ranked highly as a good by the agent; often they will be relatively insignificant, like making sure that the car is washed or the rubbish bin put out on the relevant day; sometimes they may be seen by the agent as positively bad, as, for instance, by the akratic agent who makes sure he has some cigarettes in the house even though he knows smoking is bad for him. Third, there is something more pervasive and even constitutive about ideals that marks them off from goals, and of this I shall say more later. Fourth, there is the unrealizability of ideals, a feature that most theorists who have considered the matter at all have treated as providing a vital distinction between ideals and ordinary goals or values.

This idea of unrealizability needs more attention, but first I need to say a little more about the conceptual location of the notion of an ideal. The term itself eludes tight definition since it provides a mode of description that operates on a range of other moral categories in such a way that something will be an ideal in one context and not in another. So, there is often point in contrasting ideals with obligations or duties, but this should not obscure the fact that certain sorts of obligation are close to ideals, as is illustrated by the concept of justice. Justice involves numerous duties and obligations, but it also has certain functions as an ideal. It is an obligation of justice that one pays one's taxes or does not cheat one's employer, but it is arguably part of an ideal of justice that gross income and access disparities in society should be reduced or eliminated. This prompts the thought that it is more important to explore the point of ideals discourse than to provide necessary and sufficient conditions for the applicability of the word 'ideal'. William James is a useful guide here when he says:

there must be novelty in an ideal—novelty at least for him whom the ideal grasps. Sodden routine is incompatible with ideality, although what is sodden for one person may be ideal novelty to another. This shows that there is nothing absolutely ideal: ideals are relative to the lives that entertain them. To keep out of the gutter is for us here no part of consciousness at all, yet for many of our brethren it is the most legitimately engrossing of ideals.[1]

What James calls 'novelty' provides a key to a (even the) central function of ideals discourse, though to my ear 'novelty' is not an altogether happy word for what he is getting at. We have recourse to the dimension of ideals when there is a need or impulsion to transcend our moral horizons. Hence there is a dynamism about the invocation of ideals, and hence also a relativity, as James notes, to the horizons we presently have. Without ideals, a form of the moral life might remain possible, but it would be a static affair, retaining value, but lacking vitality and direction.

Having, I hope, at least gestured helpfully at the special place occupied by talk of ideals in our moral landscape, I want to turn to the fourth feature mentioned above when distinguishing ideals from goals.

THE UNREALIZABILITY THESIS

This feature has often been described as the 'unrealizability' of ideals. They would not be ideals unless there was something 'beyond' about them, something to be striven for but not (at least readily) achieved. As my bracketed qualification suggests, there is an issue about how stringent the 'unrealizability' criterion must be. Most of those who write on the matter treat the unrealizability as absolute. James, however, sees the need for some transcendence in ideals, though he does not appear to view this as requiring absolute unrealizability. But for most philosophers, if an objective can be realized at all then it is not an ideal, however worthy of pursuit it may be. So Dorothy Emmett says (speaking particularly of Kantian-style Regulative Ideals), 'Means are used to attain ends; a Regulative Ideal is unrealisable . . .'.[2] And Nicholas Rescher agrees: 'There is inherently something unrealistic about our ideals: they are inherently incapable of "genuine fulfilment".'[3] In this matter, these writers echo Kant who says that objective realities will

---

[1] William James, 'What Makes a Life Significant', in *Talks to Teachers on Psychology: and to Students on Some of Life's Ideals* (Cambridge, Mass.: Harvard University Press, 1983), 163. I thank Nathan Tierney for directing me to this article.

[2] Dorothy Emmett, *The Role of the Unrealisable: A Study in Regulative Ideals* (New York: St Martin's Press, 1994), 3.

[3] Nicholas Rescher, *Ethical Idealism: An Inquiry into the Nature and Function of Ideals* (Berkeley and Los Angeles: University of California Press, 1987), 117.

'always fall infinitely short of actually reaching it [the ideal]'.[4] In spite of this impressive consensus, I am not entirely persuaded. Ordinary language frequently allows us to characterize existing realities as ideal; we speak of some past or current footballer as 'an ideal full back', or a politician as an ideal candidate for a particular constituency. In somewhat the same vein, we speak of the perfect candidate. Perhaps these usages are merely figurative. Possibly, we mean no more than that the people in question are very good of their kind and are getting close to the ideal. But the connection of ideals with reality arises not only in casual contexts like those mentioned, but also when we are appraising ideals themselves, in which circumstances we are often exhorted to adopt more realistic ideals. Some time ago in an issue of the Australian Broadcasting Corporation's radio programme 'Lingua Franca', the lawyer Richard Evans discussed the language of 'mission statements' put out by businesses, institutions, and professions. In the course of his discussion, Evans insisted that mission statements should not be vapid and gestural, but should contain 'achievable ideals'. We know roughly what this means, even if what it means seems in stark opposition to the unrealizability thesis.

I shall not pause for now on the linguistic issue; its point has been primarily suggestive in making the simple picture of the absolute unrealizability of ideals seem a little less obviously adequate. There is something else that complicates the simple picture, and that concerns uses of the term 'ideal' to signal a type of moral consideration that is not mandatory for all, but is realizable by some. So the Christian 'counsels of perfection' present certain ideals of living that are not thought by their proponents and adherents appropriate to the bulk of people but are for some select few. I do not want to endorse the specific aspirations mentioned in the tradition, but the various monastic ideals, such as those of poverty, chastity, and obedience were clearly regarded (rightly or wrongly) as having moral force, and as being definitely realizable, but the moral force was not sufficient to make these ideals require the adherence of all people of goodwill. Christ's discussion with the rich young man contains the basis of the distinction between counsels and commandments.[5] The young man asks what he must do to attain eternal life and Christ points out the moral

[4] Immanuel Kant, *Critique of Pure Reason*, trans. and ed. Paul Guyer and Allen W. Wood (Cambridge: Cambridge University Press, 1997), A578-B606, p. 557.
[5] Matthew 19: 16–26.

duties that he must fulfil, but when he says that he has satisfied these and will keep doing so, Christ says: 'If thou wilt be perfect, go sell what thou hast and come follow me.' The young man cannot bring himself to abandon his wealth and become a disciple, so he goes away 'sorrowing', but there is no suggestion that he has chosen wickedness over righteousness.

These ideals are demanding; indeed, too demanding to be goals for the ordinary folk, so they are, in a way, unrealizable for them.[6] Yet they remain within the reach of the select few who, contrary to the Kantian emphasis, do not fall 'infinitely short' but realize them fully, or at least seem capable of doing so. It might be objected that, for this very reason, these are not really ideals, but such a reply is, at this point, premature. Once we have explored more fully various ways of speaking of ideals, we may be in a position to locate them in relation to one another and see more clearly what force, if any, such a response has. For the moment, let us call these ideals, capacity-relative. It should be noted that the 'counsels of perfection' tend to be understood in such a way as to suggest that they can be realized by a privileged few, but the capacity-relative idea need not be deployed in so elitist a fashion. It may be that some ideals can be realized by lots of people but are beyond a small number. Whether we would then call them ideals only for the small number is another question and we will address this later.

Another important use of ideals that raises a difficulty for the unrealizability thesis is what we might call a circumstance-relative use. Here, the problem is not that there are persons, or groups of persons, who do not have sufficient capacity to measure up to the ideal, though others do; rather, the problem is that because of generally prevailing circumstances *no one* in those circumstances is presently capable of achieving the ideal. Colin Turnbull's account of the circumstances of

---

[6] This is how the counsels of perfection have often been understood, and this understanding is helpful in illustrating what I later call a 'capacity-relative' use of the term 'ideal'. Yet it should be noted that there are other, perhaps more theologically satisfactory, ways of characterizing the monastic aspirations. These avoid the suggestion that the monastic ideals are beyond the capacity of the ordinary folk. Instead, they invoke the idea of a division of spiritual labour whereby God has called different people to different roles without the suggestion that some are 'higher' than others or beyond the capacities of those who are not called to them. On this construal, the monastic requirements may not be ideals at all, but more like professional obligations which oblige those occupying a certain role without obliging those who don't.

life amongst the Ik tribe, for example, makes it plausible to say that what are elsewhere reasonably achievable moral goals are, at best, ideals for the Ik.[7] Similarly, in societies with a marked preponderance of women over men, the widespread practice of monogamy might cease to be, or never have been, an obligatory norm for those that marry at all within that society, but it might survive as an ideal for some or all of them.[8] Dire economic circumstances may make child labour a necessity in one place, even though its abolition elsewhere is morally and legally obligatory: in those dire circumstances, the abolition requirement can have the status of an ideal.

An important feature of this understanding of an ideal is that we are not relieved of attachment to the ideal by the circumstances that make it presently unrealizable. Let us call those circumstances 'defeating circumstances'. In some of the examples cited, many of the people who live in defeating circumstances might not indeed acknowledge the ideal at all; my perspective on the situations was meant to be neutral on that fact. We may think of the ideal as an ideal of outsiders who nonetheless recognize that the insiders may have no present awareness of the ideal or may indeed reject it altogether. But this is not to say that none of them will or can come to recognize it as an ideal, nor that it shouldn't be an ideal for them. Here, as with other moral categories, there is no easy route to relativism about ideals from the facts of disagreement about them. My only point here is that for those who recognize the ideal (whether they live within the defeating circumstances, or whether their standpoint is external to those circumstances) its present unrealizability shows neither that it is unrealizable *tout court* nor that it has no present implications. On the second point, the acknowledgement of the ideal should lead an agent in those defeating circumstances to do what they can to change the circumstances, or, if this is quite beyond them, to seize the opportunities provided by changes in those circumstances (however induced) to move in the direction of the ideal. And, moreover, there might reasonably be a variety of different ways of so moving. In a class-ridden society, the ideal of equality may be remote and, for a time at least, unrealizable, but there are ways of making the present situation less and less unequal.

---

[7] See Colin M. Turnbull, *The Mountain People* (New York: Simon and Schuster, 1972).

[8] I do not mean to commit myself to the view that the existence of polygamy in any given society is in fact to be explained in terms of such a preponderance of women over men.

THE GUIDANCE OF IDEALS

Let us then distinguish between capacity-relative, circumstance-relative, and absolute unrealizability and say that different ideals may involve different forms of such unrealizability. Here, for the moment, I want to leave the debate about unrealizability because there are interesting questions that arise for the role of ideals that pose themselves starkly on the assumption that ideals are absolutely unrealizable, but still arise in a somewhat different form if that assumption is relaxed. A primary one is how unrealizable states of affairs can provide any guidance for practical reason and action. Classically, the answer to this invokes a notion of approximation. We are guided by the ideal in what we feasibly do now because we can change present circumstances in the light of the ideal to bring the order of those circumstances nearer to the not fully realizable order embodied in the ideal. People often invoke some ideal of the university in this way, indeed, this is I think the best interpretation of what Newman meant when he wrote of the 'idea' of a university.[9] He was not primarily offering a semantic analysis of the word 'university' that could be defeated by pointing out that the present use of the word encompasses activities that he never envisaged or denotes institutions where the values he portrays are absent or only weakly present, but rather characterizing normative ideals that a certain sort of institution should strive to embody. Of course, there is something misleading about the picture of ideals as remote, somehow unrealizable or hardly realizable goals because their function in our lives is often more constitutive than this picture suggests. Someone who is possessed of an ideal, as we sometimes say, acts now in the light of that ideal and does not merely do certain ideal-neutral things that will bring about the ideal in some remote future. Just as with the virtues, moral agents both aim at achieving the relevant virtuous condition and in the course of doing so come actually to begin to embody the virtue, so with ideals the ideal comes to exist to a greater or lesser degree in the agent as the agent seeks to live it. The full realization of university ideals may be remote, indeed unachievable, but those who seriously hold to ideals like collegiality, truth, and intellectual freedom have already made the ideals to some degree a present reality in their lives. There is normally, in other words,

---

[9] John Henry Newman, *The Idea of a University: Defined and Illustrated,* ed. I. T. Ker (Oxford: Clarendon Press, 1976).

a non-accidental connection between the means employed to pursue an ideal and the ideal itself. I say 'normally' here in order to allow room for discussion of peculiar circumstances that might involve more contingent even paradoxical means to an ideal. It has been claimed, for instance, that there are circumstances in which an ideal of rationality might require resort to the irrational to promote it, as in the practice of nuclear deterrence. Hence at the height of the Cold War some advocates of nuclear deterrence argued that it is rational to cultivate irrationality in order to deter 'the enemy' and so bring about the rationally desired outcome of avoiding nuclear war. One form of this is getting yourself to form an intention to retaliate after a nuclear attack, even though you know it would be irrational to execute such an intention. I have the gravest doubts about the validity of such claims, but I want to allow room at least for their discussion, hence my use of 'normally'.[10] A more plausible example would be Ulysses' strategy against the Sirens where he could be said to pursue an ideal of freedom by having himself tied to the mast. But even this needs more discussion. In particular, it may be superficial to view Ulysses' tactic as an outright denial of freedom. Someone who knows they are susceptible to a certain sort of temptation may guard against it by refusing certain opportunities. So, a problem gambler might deny herself the freedom to visit casinos, even going so far as to move to another town where there were none. But, although this decision can be couched in the language of unfreedom, it is hardly a form of servility and stems from a properly managed freedom.[11]

There are indeed philosophical puzzles about the role of ideals, especially when they are understood as characterizing an end state of affairs that we are striving to bring about but realize that the end is impossible to achieve. Here are two that are raised by some remarks of Nicholas Rescher about aiming to achieve the impossible.[12] I think that Rescher clearly means his comments to bear upon the pursuit of unrealizable ideals:

1. How is it possible to act to bring about an ideal when you know that it is unrealizable?

---

[10] I have criticized these claims in 'Escaping from the Bomb', in Henry Shue (ed.), *Nuclear Deterrence and Moral Restraint: Critical Choices for American Strategy* (Cambridge: Cambridge University Press, 1989).

[11] For discussion of these sorts of problem see Jon Elster, *Ulysses and the Sirens: Studies in Rationality and Irrationality* (Cambridge and New York: Cambridge University Press, 1979).

[12] Rescher, *Ethical Idealism*, 6–7.

2. What is the point of aiming at an unrealizable ideal when you could simply aim at the realizable approximation?

A brief response to the first puzzle is that there seem to be many cases in which rational agents do set themselves consciously to strive for impossible goals. For example, a philosopher's attachment to the ideal of truth will make her strive to write a book that contains only truths and sound arguments, or at least contains only truths and sound arguments in the assertions and arguments she commits herself to, as contrasted with those of others that she considers or criticizes. Nonetheless, all philosophers know that it is impossible that all our assertions in a book will be true and arguments sound. The unrealizability of this ideal of total truth does not stand in the way of striving to achieve it. As to the second, it may, as Rescher suggests, be a significant psychological fact about people that they can reach remarkably high levels of performance by aiming at a perfection or advanced state that they know or believe to be beyond them. More of this later, but with regard to the first problem, consider an analogy with sport. In baseball, batters aim to get a hit every time they are at bat. Were they to achieve this aim comprehensively they would be hitting 1,000 (in the statistical terminology of the sport this is how perfect hitting is described; someone who gets two hits out of four times at bat is hitting 500). But everyone knows that you can't sustain this sort of record over a season, or even over a much shorter span of games. No one these days hits over 400 for a season; the last man to do so was Ted Williams of the Boston Red Sox in 1941. After the first strike-out or fly-ball, of course, the hope of 1,000 for the season is gone, but the batter still aims to hit 1,000 for the remaining games. Of course we could say that this is misleading. No batter is really aiming *at that statistic*; they merely aim to score a hit every time they go to bat. Perhaps this is more accurate, but it still means that they are aiming at what they know to be impossible. Perhaps this is still fallacious. Is there a lack of equivalence between 'Each time I go to bat, I aim to get a hit' and 'My aim is to get a hit in every venture to the plate thereby batting 1,000 for the season'? The second sentence entails the first, but the first does not obviously entail the second. If we asked someone who asserted the first sentence whether they were aiming at hitting 1,000 for the season they might quite reasonably deny it, and deny it on the grounds that such a feat is impossible. Nor does the first project set an impossible goal on each occasion that the batter steps to the plate. The question parallels one for the truth-seeking philosopher. She aims to write a true sentence each time, but does this means she aims at a book with only true sentences in it? Perhaps it is more realistic to treat her situation as strictly parallel to the baseball case. If she realizes that it is impossible to produce the all-true book, surely she would disavow the aim of doing so?

There certainly remains some unease at the idea that it could be rational for someone to aim at achieving some goal or objective that she knows or believes to be impossible to achieve. How to describe the inner directed proposal that the agent puts to herself? 'I shall bring about X though I know that it is not in my power to bring about X.' This hardly seems a possible project for a sane agent. What this shows is that the idea of agents' *intending* to do X, or even forming the intention to do X, when they know or believe that X is something they cannot do is incoherent. But is there something weaker than intending that might fit the phenomenological facts that writers like Rescher rely upon here? The word aim is perhaps ambiguous between 'intending to achieve goal X' and 'trying to achieve goal X'. Intending may involve trying but it is not the same as it. Perhaps it is more plausible to hold that we can try to do certain things that we cannot intend to do, and that amongst these is the known- (or believed)-to-be-impossible. There is an interesting parallel with those situations where the outcome of some action is not literally an impossible state of affairs but where it is not something that is in a certain sense 'within my power' to achieve. It is not impossible that a golfer should score a hole-in-one, because, apart from anything else, it is occasionally done. But the golfer's own contribution to this outcome is so minimal (though real enough) that we would, I think, rightly hesitate to say that any golfer can intend to score a hole-in-one. She can, on the other hand, *set herself* to score a hole-in-one, and *try* to score a hole-in-one, and there is plenty of behaviour that would count against the claim that she is trying to score a hole-in-one. (It won't usually help, for instance, to face in the opposite direction to the hole when playing from the tee.) The golfer who plays a safe shot short of the green because a bogey will win him the tournament, and there is danger of going in the water if you shoot for the hole, is *not* trying for a hole-in-one. Of course, there is a problem in specifying the behavioural or other differences between someone who is aiming for a hole-in-one and someone who is merely aiming to get the ball very close to the hole, and this is because aiming to get the ball very close to the hole is what you do when you are aiming to get a hole-in-one. So is there then no difference between the two? Not much, though it presumably counts as a difference on the psychological side that the agent has it in mind that a hole-in-one is needed, as when only a hole-in-one will win the tournament, or he knows there is a prize car riding on the outcome of his shot. Also, there may be reason to adopt a slightly different strategy for a hole-in-one, as when you can get close to the hole aiming either to the left or right of the flag, but every hole-in-one in the past on this green has been scored by shots landing to the right of the flag. What about aiming at something not just beyond your power, but beyond your power combined with amazing luck, namely something that is impossible. Suppose I am a police commissioner in a big city and my consuming ideal is the elimination of corruption in the large police force for which I am responsible, and suppose I believe, probably correctly, that this state of affairs can never be achieved. Am I irrational to aim at it? I am inclined to say 'no' if aim is interpreted as try for rather than intend.

It may be that much of this debate, though interesting in itself, is beside the present point. I suspect that those ideals that are unrealizable are misconceived as goals to be aimed at in this way. Instead, as suggested earlier, we should think of them as informing what we do, shedding light upon the various paths we pursue and to which they are relevant. In the Australian Labor Party, the socialist vision used to be referred to as 'the light on the hill'. The light is long since extinguished, but the metaphor could have been interpreted either as proposing something to be obtained by scaling the hill or as a source of illumination from afar of the everyday striving on the plains for a juster, fairer, and more equal society. Thinking in the first way led to talk of 'the socialist objective', but the second way of thinking *need not* encourage the idea of aiming to arrive at the peak and seizing the lamp. At most we might need to get nearer to receive more light. The second way seems to me more plausible as an account of how we tend to think of ideals in practice, or at any rate of those ideals that are fully unrealizable. If they do present a pleasing (if blurred) picture of a perfect state of affairs, then those who are attached to the ideal need not think that they must be striving to bring about exactly that state of affairs.

A further, related consideration concerning the utility of ideals is more mundane: it is often more functionally efficient to direct people to the ideal than to something more concrete and achievable well short of it. The very vagueness and 'unreality' of the ideal paradoxically may make compliance with it and guidance by it more manageable than the focus on specific reality. There is some parallel with the role of 'rough' instructions. Wittgenstein's discussion of 'Stand roughly there' comes to mind, for it is usually much more efficient to give instructions with reference to 'unreal' positions like 'there' and 'here' than to proceed with more precise direction to specifically circumscribed locations.[13] This comparison also brings out another aspect of direction by ideals which is that the relative vagueness or incompleteness of the ideal allows considerable scope for the work of practical intelligence and imagination in implementing it. This means that in complex and changing circumstances the ideal allows for flexibility and adaptation in a way that a very specific, readily realizable, blueprint will not. The fact that it is agonizingly difficult to see what the ideals of peace and justice require in circumstances like the post-apartheid South Africa is what gives so much anguished significance to the efforts of the South African Truth and Reconciliation Commission.

A final point about the guidance of ideals is that attachment to an ideal can alter widespread beliefs about what is possible and hence can change our understanding of reality. In other words, opposition to ideals quite often stems from an impoverished grasp of reality and the scope for improving it. The world of current reality and practice is interpreted conservatively and taken as canonical for determining what is possible and achievable, and hence narrow and often unimaginative limits are put upon what should be striven for. This is one of the defects of the realist opposition to ideals and the restriction of normative action to the pursuit of national interest. This is related to my earlier point about the dynamism of ideals: dedicated idealists can discover possibilities and unleash potentialities that the worldly wise and weary cannot perceive. Idealistic visionaries in Britain who brought about the abolition of the slave trade had a better grasp of the realities of power and politics than the many who believed that slavery was an entrenched part of the natural order.

THE DANGER OF IDEALS

These answers to the puzzles about the guidance of ideals lead on to an ethical anxiety about ideals. For hasn't the single-minded pursuit of an ideal proved a recipe for fanaticism? Aren't ideals destructive and

---

[13] Ludwig Wittgenstein, *Philosophical Investigations*, trans. G. E. M. Anscombe (Oxford: Basil Blackwell, 1963), 1. 88, p. 41.

damaging precisely because of their distortion of moral focus away from the achievable here and now, and because of the way that they encourage illusions about the powers, capacities, and failings of ordinary people and ordinary politicians? The key here is perhaps the word 'single-minded'. I have not been claiming that ideals are the only element in the moral life, merely a neglected element, and I would certainly want to insist that attention to ideals must take place within a context of moral obligations, other competing ideals, and a shrewd regard for what are the empirical and rational constraints on action here and now. Ideals will certainly do harm if they are implemented with disdain for central moral obligations and decencies, as was true of the implementation of the Communist ideal of the classless society (and of a version of social justice). I began by insisting on the tension between ideal and reality, and I do not want to minimize that; my point only is that we cannot ignore the importance of ideals, and we need to get a good grasp on their proper function in the moral economy. A further point is that some of the opposition to ideals comes from the damage that has been done by vicious ideals, such as the Nazi ideal of racial purification, and it is no part of my case that any ideal is a good ideal.

A further problem with the recourse to ideals in political life is that the discourse of ideals is particularly prone to some of the pitfalls of moralism discussed in Chapters 1 and 2. Both the moralism of abstraction and the moralism of deluded power are particularly pertinent to this worry. A recent set of pronouncements by British Prime Minister Tony Blair could serve as illustrations. In a speech to the World Affairs Council in Los Angeles at the end of July 2006, Mr Blair cast virtually the whole of the world's trouble spots in the light of an 'elemental' struggle about values where these were understood very much in terms of not very clearly specified ideals (presumably of democracy and freedom). This struggle was between 'our' values and those of reactionary Islam. To quote Blair:

What is happening today in the Middle East, in Afghanistan and beyond is an elemental struggle about the values that will shape our future. . . . Our values . . . represent humanity's progress throughout the ages and at each point we have had to fight for them.

Isaiah Berlin is one of the notable modern intellectuals who has highlighted the danger of ideals, especially in political life. In Berlin's paper 'The Pursuit of the Ideal' his target is more commonly 'the ideal' than 'ideals' as such but the two are sometimes hard to distinguish in his exposition, and at times he is explicitly warning about the pursuit of ideals themselves. Since an ideal is a picture of a sort of perfection, the following remark seems applicable to it, as well as to an ideal life: 'But on the other hand, the search for perfection does seem to me a recipe for bloodshed, no better even if it is demanded by the sincerest of idealists, the purest of heart.'[14] Part of his objection rests upon the point already discussed about single-mindedness, but there are other elements in his case that need to be discussed. Most centrally, there is the idea that pursuit of an ideal involves the delusional belief that the moral world is harmonious. As he puts it: 'The notion of the perfect whole, the ultimate solution, in which all good things coexist, seems to me to be not merely unattainable—that is a truism—but conceptually incoherent; I do not know what is meant by a harmony of this kind. Some among the Great Goods cannot live together.'[15]

But it is not at all clear that the pursuit of an ideal or a number of ideals must be committed to this harmony. If one recognizes restrictions of one sort or another on the attainability of some particular ideal, or some group of ideals, why should one not recognize Berlin's claim about the illusory nature of such harmony to be amongst them? It may of course be that some theorists sympathetic to ideals have held the harmony thesis; Plato may well be one of them since he holds a highly unified picture of morality. Berlin indeed thinks that most traditional moral theorists have held to a hopelessly fallacious view of morality as a concordant harmonious system of values, prohibitions, and ideals and he opposes to this what he calls value pluralism. In this, a central feature of the moral life is the possibility of profound conflict between ultimate values or between ideals. In my view there is much that is unclear about the nature of Berlin's value pluralism, although a full discussion of it is not possible here. Berlin wants to hold to a view of morality in which the fundamental values that individuals and communities have pursued are potentially in conflict within and between lives (both individual and communal). He persistently denies however that this involves any form of relativism. He is also unclear on the ways in which such conflicts are resolvable, sometimes seeming to think that they are resolvable by reason, but not by a rubric (like a utilitarian calculation or a priority ranking), and sometimes giving the impression that they are

---

[14] Isaiah Berlin, 'The Pursuit of the Ideal', in *The Proper Study of Mankind* (London: Chatto & Windus, 1997), 15.

[15] Ibid. 11.

irresolvable. There are also obscurities about how much of morality has this pluralistic feature.

In the matter of ideals, what Berlin's pluralism suggests is that ideals may be expected from time to time to clash: an ideal of equality may clash with an ideal of peace, as with the events leading to the US Civil War where the abolition of slavery seemed to require awful bloodshed, or an ideal of liberty may clash with an ideal of social justice, as when speech may have to be restricted because of the damage it will do to the rights of oppressed groups. Here I am thinking of cases where ideals are fully shared by those concerned but the conflict remains. How then are such conflicts to be resolved? It seems to me that there is no point in simply throwing up one's hands and appealing to emotion, even if there is no simple algorithm for reaching a solution. Nor indeed does Berlin think as much for he supports trade-offs, whereby 'rules, values, principles must yield to each other in varying degrees in specific situations' leading to 'a precarious equilibrium' that wards off 'desperate situations' and 'intolerable choices'.[16] This looks like reason at work even if the details are somewhat obscure.

Some such clashes may involve an element of the tragic, but in the case of ideals a resolution will usually not involve the outright denial or abandonment of an ideal. In this respect the conflict of ideals seems to differ from a clash of obligations. Where significant obligations conflict, we can have moral dilemmas or what are often called 'dirty hands' situations. In the former, whatever the agent does is wrong and there is no right answer to his or her dilemma; in the latter, both choices are wrong but one is deemed 'necessary'. In either case, the resolution seems to involve one in wrongdoing, in the violation of an obligation. Much remains to say about moral dilemmas and dirty hands, and I shall say some of it in the next chapter. But, in the case of ideals, we seem characteristically to face postponement rather than outright violation of our ideal. In fighting a legitimate war, for instance, realization of the ideal of liberty, or certain aspects of it, may have to be deferred in the interests of communal defence. So, a certain degree of censorship may have to be tolerated by the lovers of liberty. Or in the event of a natural disaster like a flood or hurricane, the liberty of citizens may have to be restricted for a time in order to bring adequate help to victims. No doubt, with a bit of ingenuity, some of these sorts of examples can be seen as indirect promotions of the ideal in question as in war the

---

[16] Ibid. 15.

temporary imposition of censorship may contribute to preserving the longer-term liberties of citizens against an enemy whose success would mean a greater decrease in liberty, but this is not always plausible, as it is not indeed plausible in the case of disaster relief.

What these examples do further suggest is that the ideal that must yield to the circumstances or to the demands of a different ideal remains operative. The agent who adheres to the ideal is still vigilant to its requirements, so that curtailments or compromises are kept to a minimum and strivings to implement it are resumed when appropriate. Those who constantly compromise on their ideals are at serious risk of paying mere lip-service to them, and this is of course the serious moral charge implicit in the widespread complaints of 'pragmatism' levelled so often against contemporary politicians. Tony Blair is an interesting case, a complex politician who has been accused of both pragmatism and moralistic idealism, though not in connection with the same policies. When in Opposition, Blair was a ferocious opponent of Thatcherism, a stern critic of the free market, and an advocate of unilateral removal of all nuclear weapons from British soil. In Government, his distance from Mrs Thatcher reduced dramatically as he morphed into a supporter of markets, privatization, and the independent deterrent.[17] This transformation may show great flexibility of mind, or the effects of a Damascus moment of political conversion, but, on a less charitable interpretation, seems to indicate a decidedly loose attachment to the ideals vehemently announced beforehand.

Where ideals are genuinely held, their controlling role has every claim to be regarded as an exercise of reason. It would indeed be unreasonable to claim adherence to an ideal and not use it to regulate behaviour in this and other ways. But is reason exercised in the decision to choose to suspend pursuit of one ideal in the interests of another where they clash? Heeding Berlin-type objections to a rubric or mechanism for deciding such matters, we should still, I believe, hold that it is. Certainly, those who face a choice between ideals of peace and justice do not simply respond as if tossing a coin would be all right, nor do they merely yield to emotional gusts this way or that; rather, they try to act in a way that seems appropriate to the situation, respects consistency, and can be defended in discussion with critics. This is not to deny that some

---

[17] For a trenchant review of the progress of Mr Blair's ideals see ch. 9, 'Right is the New Left', in Francis Wheen's *How Mumbo-Jumbo Conquered the World: A Short History of Modern Delusions* (London: Fourth Estate, 2004).

decisions of this sort can be agonizing, and can seem right but be difficult to explain or defend. But our thinking is prone to such encumbrances in every domain, not merely in the realm of ideals.

RELATIVISM AND IDEALS

I said before that there was no easy way to relativism about ideals, but even if some ideals are rationally recommendable to any moral agent, it may be that some relativity does attach to ideals (other than the capacity and circumstantial relativity discussed earlier). In this section, I will explore the complex issue of how much relativity attaches to ideals. My point of departure will be the appealing thought that the moral role of ideals is peripheral to a more central, core morality. This has been an abiding thought in moral philosophy though its different expressions suggest somewhat different interpretations of the thought's meaning. So, Adam Smith distinguishes between justice and 'the other virtues' by comparing justice to 'the rules of grammar' that preserve language as an instrument of communication, whereas the other virtues are more like the loose, vague rules for 'what is sublime and elegant in composition' aiming thereby to give us 'a general idea of the perfection we ought to aim at, than afford us any certain and infallible directions of acquiring it'.[18] In P. F. Strawson's influential paper 'Social Morality and Individual Ideal',[19] he draws a contrast between the morality of duty, obligation, and right which he sees as essentially required by the existence of social life and its institutions, roles, and civic requirements, and the way that individuals shape their own lives and destinies in the space left to them by the silence of social morality. Though Strawson does not commit himself to anything as explicit as a social contract theory of morality there is certainly an echo of that tradition in his demarcation of social morality from the ethic of individual ideal. Indeed, more committed contractarians, such as Tim Scanlon, treat ideals in a similar way. For both Strawson and Scanlon, the picture is one in which stringent moral requirements are imposed in a core area of morality ('what we owe to each other' as Scanlon has it) but less demanding, and differently justified, moral features, most typically ideals, fall outside of that.

---

[18] Adam Smith, *The Theory of Moral Sentiments,* ed. D. D. Raphael and A. L. Macfie (Oxford: Clarendon Press, 1976), III. 6. 11, pp. 175–6.
[19] *Philosophy: The Journal of the Royal Institute of Philosophy,* 36 (1961), 1–17.

Any such demarcation surely has difficulties if it purports to separate ideals from more quotidian morality by the contrast of individual aspiration with social requirement. At the simplest level, it is clear that ideals can be communal possessions (as I have assumed earlier), but perhaps Strawson does not mean to deny this. There is nothing in what he says that rules out an ideal held by one individual becoming persuasive for others and their adopting it for themselves. Perhaps the point is rather that where a number of people share an ideal, they do so essentially *as* individuals, whereas any office-holder has the duties he or she has because of the office, citizens have the rights they have as citizens, and so on. But this too seems to distort reality. Many ideals held by a group of people are held as communal and go some way towards defining what it is to be an individual who is located in that community. Some of Strawson's comments acknowledge this, though others seem in tension with it.

It may be that the social/individual contrast made by Strawson really stands misleading proxy for a rather different contrast between stringency and optionality. The treatment of ideals as individual and obligations and the like as social may embody the idea that ideals are not demanded of individuals and cannot be socially or legally enforced. This connects with certain liberal outlooks that seek to remove both legal and social sanctions from some types of morality. Even such a fan of ideals as Nicholas Rescher thinks that 'Ideals lack the sort of universality we attribute to norms; there is something more particularized, more parochial about them.'[20] And he adds, 'A person who subscribes to certain ideals accordingly has no right to expect that others will do so as well . . .'.[21] On the other hand, it seems that a liberal society itself cannot exist without general adherence to certain ideals, most notably the ideal of liberty, but also certain ideals associated with the rule of law, such as impartiality and equality. In this connection, it is worth noting that Lon Fuller, the American legal philosopher, has made much of a distinction between the morality of duty and the morality of aspiration, and although he does not explicitly talk of ideals, he links the morality of aspiration to the seeking of perfection, listing eight 'excellences' that the law should strive to instantiate.[22] Fuller's account of the distinction is not altogether clear. One criterion he uses is the way penalties and blame are attached to violations of duty but not to failures in the

---

[20] Rescher, *Ethical Idealism*, 122.   [21] Ibid. 123.
[22] Lon L. Fuller, *The Morality of Law* (New Haven: Yale University Press, 1977).

pursuit of aspirations, whereas rewards and praise go to those who live up to aspirations but are inappropriate to those who merely do their duty. Plausible as it sounds at first, I am not sure that this test will do; after all, we sometimes do praise those who do their duty, and often criticize those whose behaviour fails to match their professed ideals. And someone may be blamed, and blamed severely, not only for failing to live up to ideals they have embraced, but for failing to have certain ideals at all. But whatever the inadequacies of Fuller's definitions, it is worth noting here his attempt to ground law upon both the morality of aspiration and that of duty.

Inasmuch as social roles are important for social morality (as Strawson insists) then the significance of ideals in the operation of such roles and the functioning of institutions in which they are embedded cannot be ignored, and his contrast tends to obscure this fact. He does see an important link between social morality and individual ideal in that the stability provided by social morality makes the pursuit of individual ideals possible, and admits that there is more to say about the complexity of the relations between 'minimal' morality and ideals, but he does not develop important links that go in the other direction. Consider, for instance, the way in which the ideal of truth itself conditions (or should condition) the roles of academics in universities, the ideal of caring the role of nurses, the ideal of justice the role of judges. There is indeed a complex issue about the relation of ideals to duties, obligations, etc. in such institutional settings, but the issue is mostly obscured by the sharpness of the Strawsonian contrast. I suspect that a full exploration of the relation would pay close attention to the way in which the concept of ethos operates to connect ideals and duties. We cannot address this matter here, but enough has been said to show some of the inadequacies of Strawson's emphases.

But the issue of relativity remains, though, as always, there are many ambiguities surrounding talk of relativism. The discussion of Strawson suggests that the common move of treating all ideals as invariably less universally demanding, as somehow more optional, than the obligations of 'minimal morality' obscures too much. Ideals such as justice, peace, and equality are misunderstood, and underestimated, if they are seen as optional commitments on all fours with the ideals of display that inspired Regency dandies or the ascetic ideals of monks. Though there can be much dispute about their meaning, the former ideals have claims to universal adoption in a way that the latter do not and they can inform and change the operations of the minimal morality. Consider the way that the ideal of equality has been invoked to such effect in the last fifty years or so in altering the 'minimal morality' sphere of obligation with respect to the treatment of women. But when this is allowed, there may be still be important areas of relativity and optionality within the conceptual space of ideals. Here are some:

One form of relativity concerns the degree of attachment to an ideal or, perhaps better, the personal priority that it has with different individuals or the social priority with different communities. Some of Berlin's ambiguous relation with full-blooded relativism stems from his awareness of this very different sort of relativity. What I have in mind here is that although the ideal of truth, for instance, has an objective claim to the attention of all, it may have a special role in the lives of intellectuals, just as the ideal of justice must concern everyone, but have a special significance for judges.

Another form of relativity concerns the way in which some ideals may be profoundly important for some people but quite legitimately of little or no concern at all to others. Think, for instance, of the ideal of sartorial elegance or of physical fitness. These are not perhaps what many would think of as moral ideals, and that, of course, raises important questions about the demarcation of morality from other normative areas. This is too big an issue to settle here, but certainly the ideal of supreme physical fitness, as that of sartorial elegance, can exercise a dominating influence in the ordering of one individual's life, as indeed of a community's, without that meaning that it must do so for others. In an area more significantly moral, certain religious ideals may evoke respect, even a degree of admiration, in a wider community without the outsiders seeing any need to adopt them. I am thinking of such ideals as those of asceticism where the inability to share the ideal may relate to deep differences in belief about God or about what is important in life. These religious examples shade into such religious and non-religious ones as invoke the concept of the supererogatory, as with vocational ideals of self-sacrifice and service beyond a normal sense of duty. Then there are others that are less clear as with Strawson's example of the ideals of personal honour that may have a profound grip on members of a military caste. I am not altogether sure what he has in mind, but one possibility might encompass such behaviour as that of the soldier who courts certain death by falling upon an unexploded grenade in order to save the lives of his comrades. This would be admirable but supererogatory were an ordinary civilian to do it for other civilians, but it may have more pressing force in the military context without quite being an obligation. In any case, in that context, it is perfectly intelligible to those who are not bound by such an imperative and they can see the moral force of the reasons behind it. These ideals of honour and service may be specialized in some respects, but they are not beyond the scope of reason and can make sense outside of the military context. For other ideals of honour not only can we imagine them as open to rational appraisal by others, but indeed to rational rejection. The duelling code of honour is an example and there may be other 'honour' elements that embody dangerous forms of romanticism about violence. Something similar may be true of Scanlon's discussion of the ideal of patriotism. He thinks those with patriotic ideals and those with incompatible ideals of 'individual independence' should respect each other though separated in an important way. But this seems to mislocate the problem: it is not one concerning the bases of personal respect, but one concerning the reasons for accepting or rejecting the ideals themselves.[23] The ideals call for reasoned engagement rather than isolating respect.

I do not want to be dogmatic either way on these relativities and a great deal will depend on the examples cited; I merely want to tilt the balance away from the prevailing view of optionality that seems to suggest too easy a resort to the arbitrary or subjective. Certainly, the possibility should at least be considered that some of the matters that have been regarded in the light of binding imperatives upon all should be viewed rather as dominating ideals for many, attractive for others, but not even morally relevant to other good people. Perhaps lifelong marital commitments (for those who are serious sexual partners) should fall into this category. Jane Sullivan, a journalist in the Melbourne newspaper *The Age,* seemed to have something of this sort in mind when writing of the ebb and flow of romantic 'relationships'. She says: 'While one perfect lifelong romantic relationship is still the ideal, relationships end and new ones start all the time—and no-one is really surprised to find out that sometimes the new relationships overlap with the old. We don't exactly approve of "adultery", but we accept it, not as an evil abstraction but as a fact of life, something couples have to sort out between themselves.'[24]

If this sort of suggestion is to be taken seriously, it adds another dimension to the discussion of unrealizability and takes our earlier

---

[23] T. M. Scanlon, *What We Owe to Each Other* (Cambridge, Mass.: Harvard University Press, 1998), 346.

[24] Jane Sullivan, 'We're Still Silly over Sex', *The Age* (26 Dec. 1998), 6.

discussion of 'counsels of perfection' a step further. This is because the case of marriage is one in which the commitment to marital fidelity is certainly realizable (and realized) by many of those who get married, but those who do not realize it, are often treated as falling short of an ideal rather than as violating binding duties. Not everyone is prepared to concede as much, and this shows that there can be room for debate about the stringency of requirements of ideals or even about whether certain moral values count as ideals or not. G. K. Chesterton highlights this point of controversy with some unsympathetic ridicule: 'Unfortunately, on the theoretic side, the word "ideal" is far from being an exact term, and is open to two almost opposite interpretations. For many would say that marriage is an ideal as some would say that monasticism is an ideal, in the sense of a counsel of perfection. Now certainly we might preserve a conjugal ideal in this way. A man might be reverently pointed out in the street as a sort of saint, merely because he was married. A man might wear a medal for monogamy; or have letters after his name similar to V.C. or D.D.; let us say L.W. for "Lives With His Wife," or N.D.Y. for "Not Divorced Yet." '[25]

CROOKED TIMBER?

There is another aspect of the role of ideals that I must address, and it is explicitly raised by Berlin. He often invokes the stirring, if somewhat mysterious, sentence from Immanuel Kant: 'Out of the crooked timber of humanity no straight thing was ever made.' Berlin takes this to be a clarion call against the demand that human beings strive for perfection or seek after the ideal; human nature is not the sort of thing that can be 'made straight'. But this can be interpreted in at least two ways. One is as a reminder of the trite, though sometimes forgotten, fact that we human beings are fallible, errant, sometimes perverse and vicious creatures. This is what we might call the *modest* reading of the remark. But there is also what we might call the *extreme* reading which holds more dramatically that humanity is inherently depraved and deluded. These correspond to two classical theological interpretations of the doctrine of original sin.

The modest and the extreme readings are important for the assessment of Berlin-style objections to the role of ideals. Where the idea is that

---

[25] G. K. Chesterton, *The Superstition of Divorce* (London: Chatto and Windus, 1920), 133–4.

human nature cannot sustain a positive role for ideals, then it is only the extreme version that gives it any plausible support. Where the suggestion is that human beings are either incapable of striving after ideals or capable of doing so but certain to produce massive harm by their efforts, then the extreme reading may help to show that our incapacities and depraved proclivities support the suggestion. But it is hardly supported by the modest reading, and I would argue that the modest reading, or something like it, is more plausibly sustained by the recorded history of our species. To say this much is not to be particularly optimistic about the species, for our grim record of savagery is certainly depressing, but it is to register the significance not only of sanctity and heroism, but of all the unremarkable ordinary goodness that is a basis for taking the possibility of the enterprise of ethics seriously at all.

Yet it may be objected that there is something in human nature, short of depravity and intellectual incompetence, that makes it difficult and dangerous to pursue ideals sensibly. This 'something' involves the ever-present problem of being realistic about the implementation of the ideal. When attempts to approximate the ideal are confronted by stubborn realities that seem to require action at odds with the ideal, we are strongly tempted to stick to the demands of the ideal in ways that so clash with reality that they produce not just sub-optimal but downright bad outcomes. In such situations as Voltaire once put it: 'the best is the enemy of the good'.[26] This is one of the things that so worries the realist critics of idealism in foreign affairs. Earlier I mentioned ways of responding to a variety of clashes between ideal and reality, but the present suggestion is that there is bound to be a strong temptation endemic to the business of pursuing an ideal to ignore realities or in other ways allow the grip of the ideal to distort our practical reasoning and responding. At the level of public policy, we could cite the policy of school bussing whereby children from various neighbourhoods were transported considerable distances from their homes to produce schools with an appropriate mix of pupils. The policy was motivated by an ideal of racial equality, but ignored the psychological, social, and educational barriers to its feasible implementation. Or to take a rather different type of distortion, one at the level of personal character rather than public policy, we might consider the sort of character fault that we name 'perfectionism' whereby people are unable to achieve anything (of the relevant kind) because they will only settle for the ideal. Again

---

[26] Voltaire, 'Dramatic Art', in *Philosophical Dictionary* (1764).

both examples are real enough but provide warnings about the misuse of ideals rather than arguments that such distortions are inevitable. Idealists are not bound to suffer from debilitating perfectionism, nor are social policies in pursuit of an ideal bound to be insensitive to circumstances. The pursuit of an ideal will run certain risks and the present objection can be seen as usefully providing suggestions about what these are, but it does not show that the risks are never worth taking. Moreover, objections that focus on the dangerous unrealism of ideals consistently ignore the ways in which commitment to ideals can radically transform our sense of what is possible. Realists in the past were constantly telling us that all sorts of things were impossible that idealists then helped to bring about, such as the abolition of slavery, the emancipation of women, and the internal peaceful overthrow of communist tyranny.

There is another difficulty for ideals which is not as commonly noticed, and which is in a way the obverse of the objection above. This is the problem created by idealizing existing realities: seeing them as already embodying the ideal when they are very far from it. This is a particular temptation for conservative thinkers where the existing realities are the result of tradition. So it can happen that ideals associated with the family or the police or the church exercise such an appeal that they blind people to the far grimmer realities of such institutions here and now. There does seem to be a marked human tendency towards such idealizing, but again it is a tendency that is there to be overcome. Moreover, it is there to be overcome with the help of the ideal itself. The idealizing distortion needs to be brought face to face with the divergence that exists between reality and ideal. Spousal and child abuse do not show that ideals of family love, devotion, and care are not worth having, but that they need to be enacted rather than merely rhetorically invoked.

Let me make a further point about the link between human nature and ideals by way of conclusion. In discussions of business ethics and of regulatory regimes for both business and the professions, it used to be common to support either heavy regulation or an appeal to self-interest by recourse to the slogan that we should 'economize on virtue'. The idea was that we could expect to get much further in promoting the good in commerce or the professions by arranging things so that it was in the self-interest of the human beings and institutions concerned to do the right thing. But increasingly, it has been argued against this that economizing on virtue runs the risk of destroying the legitimate bases on which virtue can work. If people are viewed as incapable of virtue, then that is how they will view themselves, and so a potentially powerful tool for institutional and personal improvement will be lost. Something similar can be said of the idea that we should 'economize on ideals'. Indeed, the question of human nature, raised by Berlin's comments, leads naturally to questions about the moral psychology of ideals. In particular, there is the relation of ideals to hope. In classic medieval treatments, such as Aquinas's, hope is dealt with as a theological virtue, but there is, at least phenomenologically, a natural equivalent of it concerning the appropriate attitude to take towards the world and human life considered as oriented towards the future, and this seems to be the province of hope, and despair. Ideals play a part in sustaining hope, just as hope itself seems to generate ideals. But at the verge of this interesting extension of our topic I must stop.

4

Engagement in Evil: Politics, Dirty Hands, and Corruption

'If there is a commonplace in morals, it is that power and greatness corrupt men . . .'

Joseph de Maistre, *Considerations on France*

In the film documentary 'The Fog of War', the former US Secretary of Defence, Robert McNamara was interviewed at length about his career in politics and elsewhere, with particular reference to his thoughts on the prosecution of the Vietnam War. McNamara was an enthusiastic 'hawk' who now presents his enthusiasm as more qualified and muted, but admits to many errors of judgement about the war. In the course of the interview he enunciates a list of principles for the conduct of foreign policy of which rule number 9 is: 'In order to do good, you must engage in evil'.

McNamara studied philosophy and politics at Berkeley and this comment suggests he must have been an admirer of Machiavelli. Note that he does not say: 'In order to do good you must engage *with* evil' or 'In order to do good, you must *do* evil'. The crucial phrase is 'engage in'. I think this is a crucial phrase for the discussion of evil-doing in politics in a good cause or what is sometimes called 'dirty hands' or with a somewhat different connotation 'noble cause corruption'. McNamara is obviously not merely making the point that involvement in politics, especially international politics, will require confrontation with evil, but nor is he only making the more controversial point that you must do the occasional evil act. The use of the word 'engage' strongly suggests a more ongoing commitment to evil-doing than the occasional act of evil, and McNamara's record in power reinforces what might otherwise seem a debatable point of linguistic interpretation. McNamara's rule, formulated for an earlier era of United States confrontation with distant foreigners, finds an echo in much that is written and thought today in the USA and elsewhere about the requirements of 'doing good' in foreign affairs. Michael Ignatieff, for instance, in a newspaper article, reprinted in the Melbourne *Age* from the *New York Times Magazine*, argued that the United States may have to 'traffic in evil' in order to defeat the evil of terrorism.[1] Under the heading 'It's Time to Fight Dirty', Ignatieff discussed the need for desperate measures that he believed the September 11 attacks on the USA might well now license. In particular, he discussed the moral validity of resort to assassination, torture, and other rights violations that might be required to defeat the terrorists.

I don't know if Ignatieff supplied the heading for this article (his subsequent book from which this is an excerpt is called, less dramatically, 'The Lesser Evil' and is distinctly critical of many proposals to fight terrorism by soiled means) but the 'dirty' reference recalls recent philosophical debates about political morality that have gone under the title of 'dirty hands'. These have been given new life by the outrage of September 11 and the subsequent 'war on terrorism'. The primary contemporary treatment of the topic is Michael Walzer's. In his influential article 'Political Action: The Problem of Dirty Hands', he coined the term 'dirty hands' adapting it from Jean Paul Sartre's play of the same name.[2] But the idea has a more ancient lineage, dating back to Machiavelli's treatment of political methods in *The Prince* and *The Discourses,* and drawing upon elements in Thomas Hobbes and Max Weber. I call it 'the idea', but there are many different ideas that converge under the heading of 'dirty hands'. The tradition of political realism that I discussed in my first two chapters has affinities with the dirty hands doctrine, and some intellectual ancestry in common, but (as I said there) it is better to treat them separately. Roughly speaking, realism argues for a dominant amoralism in foreign affairs where dirty hands refers to the necessity of an explicitly acknowledged immoralism. Of course, I argue that realists are confused about what they intend and should more charitably be interpreted, especially in their negative ideas, as criticizing the place of moralism, not morality, in foreign affairs, but there is no denying that much of their explicit assertion is propounding a wide-ranging amoralism.

---

[1] Michael Ignatieff, 'It's Time to Fight Dirty', *The Age*, Melbourne (29 May 2004).
[2] Michael Walzer, 'Political Action: The Problem of Dirty Hands', *Philosophy and Public Affairs*, 2/2 (1973).

A further issue in the discussion of political morality concerns the level of the moral problematic that is addressed. There are many different types of potential 'immoralities' that can cause concern, ranging at one end from the limiting of time for the exercise of moral sympathy and the coarsening of sensitivities—what we might call, following Bernard Williams, moral misdemeanours, or even moral inconveniences—to moral crimes at the other end of the spectrum.[3] In my discussion I shall be dealing for the most part with the heavy end of the spectrum.

I want to explore the dirty hands debate beginning with an analysis of the structure of Michael Walzer's influential but I believe rather confusing position. I then want to move to more substantive issues by examining the problems in thinking of politics in the way suggested by Walzer and by other, even more permissive, authors. This will take me into a discussion of the concept of corruption and to certain puzzles about 'noble corruption'. Before embarking on the complexities of the philosophical discussion of the merits and demerits of 'engaging in evil' in certain circumstances, it is worth noting that the real-world context for dirty tricks and dirty hands commonly involves much cruder and more degenerate calculations and violations of the moral order than are usually envisaged by the philosophers. The history of the CIA's covert operations, recently skilfully explored by Tim Weiner, makes it clear that gross moral violations, including murder, fraud, initiating illegal wars and revolutions, and persistently deceiving one's own political leadership, can all be laid at the door of the CIA. Nor is it probable that the secret manipulations and excursions of other nations' intelligence organizations are much cleaner. The idealized conditions invoked by the philosophers of dirty hands are often comically remote from the reasoning and psychology of the spooks and politicians that actually get their hands, arms, and shoulders dirty. The CIA operatives who decided to overthrow President Mossadeq of Iran and install the Shah in 1953 or those agents who, apparently emboldened by the 'success' of their Persian adventure, overturned the government of Guatamala in 1954, all thought that their sowing of death and corruption was legitimated by its part in stemming the supreme evil of communism. In fact, as Weiner demonstrates in depressing detail, their judgements regarding people, culture, ideology, and consequences were uninformed, thoughtless, and hubristic. Nonetheless, their attitudes and actions helped sustain or

---

[3] Bernard Williams, 'Politics and Moral Character', in Stuart Hampshire (ed.), *Public and Private Morality* (Cambridge: Cambridge University Press, 1978).

create an atmosphere in which more of the same became part of the normative fabric of the organization and its covert operations. The philosophical defenders of dirty hands would, of course, decry any analogy between their scenarios and these real-world events, but the issuing of theoretical licences for grave immorality in idealized political contexts cannot be viewed in complete isolation from the way political agents actually behave. I shall return to this theme at the conclusion of this chapter.

THE CONCEPTUAL STRUCTURE OF DIRTY HANDS

The philosophical dirty hands position is more accommodating of the claims of morality than realism and, at the same time, more challenging of them. Herein lies its somewhat paradoxical nature. In Walzer's hands, for instance, the basic thesis is that we need morally good politicians who will generally allow morality to guide their thinking, though there are certain circumstances in which the politician must violate the deepest constraints of morality. In doing so, the politician should remain conscious that he or she has acted immorally, even though in some sense rightly. In such circumstances, politicians face a tragic choice, but it is not a moral dilemma in the technical philosophical sense. A moral dilemma is where there is no right answer to the choice the agent faces and where doing X or not doing X are equally morally wrong. In the dirty hands scenario we are asked to believe that doing X is morally wrong and yet it is palpably right to do it. As Walzer has more recently written of his own position, it is both 'provocative and paradoxical'.[4]

There are various ways of resolving or defusing the paradox, though Walzer is, I think, anxious to let it stand. This is partly because he thinks there are two important but potentially irreconcilable strands in our moral thinking which he usually characterizes as deontological-absolutist as against utilitarian, and here there is an echo of Max Weber's opposition in 'Politics as Vocation' between 'an ethic of ultimate ends' and 'an ethic of responsibility'. Although the terms in which Weber frames the contrast tend to confuse rather than clarify the issues, it is probable that one thing he has in mind for the 'ultimate ends' side of

---

[4] See Michael Walzer, 'Emergency Ethics', ch. 3 in his *Arguing About War* (New Haven and London: Yale University Press, 2004), 33.

the conflict is an ethic involving absolute prohibitions which he sees as in tension with an outlook more geared to counting consequences. As Weber puts it: 'there is an abysmal contrast between conduct that follows the maxim of an ethic of ultimate ends—that is, in religious terms, "the Christian does rightly and leaves the results with the Lord"—and conduct that follows the maxim of an ethic of responsibility, in which case one has to give an account of the foreseeable results of one's action'.[5] The starkness of this contrast is one source of confusion since absolutists are not totally indifferent to consequences—not all their ethic consists of absolute prohibitions—and non-absolutists need not be obsessed only with consequences. But Weber is adamant that it is impossible in politics to adhere generally to the absolutist ethic of ultimate ends, largely because of the central role of violence in politics.

Understandably, some theorists have been impatient with Walzer's position. One reaction is to declare it a simple contradiction and resolve the air of paradox by insisting that morality is concerned with what it is right to do, all-things-considered, and therefore if it is right to torture a suspected terrorist in a 'ticking bomb' situation (as Walzer believes) then that is no violation of morality, for it is the moral thing to do.[6] Often enough, and curiously enough, Walzer seems to agree. When he defends the decision to violate the deep prohibition, say on torture or on bombing innocent non-combatants in certain circumstances, he does so by invoking certain values that he takes to be overwhelming and that have a powerful moral flavour to them. This comes out in his discussions of 'supreme emergency' which is a category that he devises to give an explanation of the circumstances that can justify dirtying the hands. So he says, in his most recent discussion of supreme emergency, that the need for dirty hands arises when 'our deepest values are radically at risk' and 'a certain kind of utilitarianism reimposes itself', this being 'the utilitarianism of extremity' set against 'a rights normality'.[7]

It is surely plausible to see this as the claim that superior moral considerations of a distinctively political kind have defeated other moral considerations that would more normally be compelling. This seems especially clear when Walzer goes on to spell out the overwhelming value protected by extremity utilitarianism, namely the value of the moral

---

[5] Max Weber, 'Politics as Vocation', in *From Max Weber: Essays in Sociology*, ed. H. H. Gerth and C. Wright Mills (London: Routledge and Kegan Paul, 1977), 120.

[6] Kai Neilson takes this approach in his 'There Is No Dilemma of Dirty Hands', *South African Journal of Philosophy*, 15/1 (1996), 1–7.

[7] Walzer, 'Emergency Ethics', 40.

community. 'Moral communities make great immoralities morally possible,' he declares.[8] But this can only mean that the great immoralities are immoral only elsewhere, since here they are permissible because morally possible. Indeed, Walzer's considered position is not that they are merely morally possible but morally necessary. In addition, there is a non-utilitarian flavour to the way Walzer spells out the distinctive pull upon the politician to violate the moral constraints. This pull is the pull of role morality, and it arises from Walzer's notably duty-oriented understanding of the political leader's role. Here, Walzer's thinking is closely connected with the tradition of political realism, though his emphasis is usually closer to communitarian rather than simply statist perspectives. He does not identify the political community and the state, but he views the state as the natural instrument serving political community. He goes so far as to speak of a 'fit' that usually obtains between political community and state and is mediated by shared history and culture, though this idea is less emphatic in more recent writings.[9] The statesmen (or women) and the military leadership are the figures that Walzer concentrates upon in considering supreme emergency. In the analysis in *Just and Unjust Wars*, he insists that political rulers are obliged by their roles to put the safety of their community (in circumstances of supreme emergency) ahead of their 'absolute' moral obligations not to torture or to kill the innocent. As he says later: 'No government can put the life of the community and all its members at risk, so long as there are actions available to it, even immoral actions, that would avoid or reduce the risk. . . . That is what political leaders are for; that is their first task.'[10] Furthermore, the significance of this task is cashed out in terms of the supreme value of 'moral community'. When the continuity, the 'ongoingness', of a community's way of life is threatened then the prospect is that of 'a loss greater than any that can be imagined, except for the destruction of humanity itself'.[11]

This version of the dirty hands story brings Walzer much closer to the impatient critic's position, and, incidentally, further away from the

---

[8] Ibid. 50.

[9] Compare the emphasis in 'The Moral Standing of States: A Response to Four Critics', *Philosophy and Public Affairs*, 9/3 (1980), 209–29, to that in 'Emergency Ethics'. The flavour of Walzer's 'fit' can be gathered from the following quotation which appears in the earlier article: 'Indeed, the history, culture, and religion of the community may be such that authoritarian regimes come, as it were, naturally, reflecting a widely shared world view or way of life', 224–5.

[10] Walzer, 'Emergency Ethics', 42.   [11] Ibid. 43.

supposed triumph of a version of utilitarianism. Not only is the violation of the deep moral prohibitions accomplished *within* morality, but it is done by invoking a powerful version of role morality whereby the ruler is absolutely prohibited by the role and the supreme value it serves from ever refraining from acts that can protect the moral community's way of life from risk of extinction. This prohibition obtains no matter how immoral those acts otherwise would be. This doesn't seem like any form of utilitarianism, even though it involves assessment of risks. It also removes his position from that sometimes attributed to Machiavelli, and popular in some philosophical circles today, that there are necessities beyond morality that should override its dictates. In Walzer's original article, there were definite elements of this, but in his developed view, it is morality itself that overrides the deepest constraints.

With one significant qualification to be discussed shortly, Walzer's dirty hands position seems to collapse into a dramatic version of what Thomas Nagel has called 'threshold deontology' or what I have called elsewhere 'balanced exceptionalism'. This view is associated with the intuitionist tradition, but has an influence beyond that. The basic idea is that what it is morally right to do is often straightforward but is sometimes the outcome of a process of balancing obligations (or the demands of values, virtues, etc.) that are none of them absolutely binding as they stand. In the intuitionist framework, for instance, there are a number of prima facie duties that can come into conflict and, when they do, the weightier will prevail in determining the right thing to do. This seems to be a plausible way of viewing Walzer's dirty hands decision, with the proviso that the prima facie obligation not to torture or attack the innocent is very powerful in the scales to the point where it can only be overridden by the weightiest of considerations, those of supreme emergency. But there is a qualification, which is that, for Walzer, the overriding remains somehow a wrongdoing, whereas for the balanced exceptionalist no wrong can be attributed to you if you have done the balancing conscientiously.[12] There may be a sense of regret that one cannot avoid doing something that was prima facie wrong—it would be more comfortable if one's prima facie duties did not conflict and

---

[12] The influential intuitionist W. D. Ross does indeed recognize that there can be a sort of residue effect of the fact that a prima facie duty has been overruled. Since we still recognize the prima facie duty as such, then we may feel 'compunction' at not being able to fulfil it but 'not indeed shame or repentance'. And, in some cases, we may have some further duty to make up 'somehow' for the right decision not to heed the prima facie duty. Ross, *The Right and the Good* (Oxford: Clarendon Press, 1930), 28.

therefore need resolution, but you are not a wrongdoer. The granting of exemption from the prohibition on intentionally killing or torturing the innocent is part of a normal, even routine, business of balancing presumptive obligations in order to find what is finally obligatory or prohibited. If the scales tell you that it is morally permitted or even morally obligatory intentionally to kill or torture the innocent, then in these circumstances it cannot be wrong to do so.[13]

We may well think that Walzer shows more sensitivity to the horror of what must be done by the conscientious ruler, and that the balanced exceptionalist's statement of the case is too bland, and insufficiently registers the psychological reactions appropriate to the deeds required by supreme emergency. Nonetheless, the position seems to provide a simpler framework than Walzer's own for stating what his view amounts to. But much turns on whether the 'moral remainder', as some philosophers have called the focus of these psychological attitudes of regret or remorse, is better accounted for by some mechanism other than an insistence that the agent has really done wrong in doing right. Walzer's paradox may better register the state of character of the agent who has been brought to violate a deep moral norm and provide a greater incentive to extricate from the dirty hands situation. It is worth quoting a description from someone who was faced with an extreme moral crisis: the prisoner doctor Olga Lengyel who found herself administering poison to newborn babies in Auschwitz in order to protect their mothers since every woman with a child in tow was thereby marked for death. Lengyel said of herself: 'I marvel to what depths these Germans made us descend . . . The Germans succeeded in making murderers of even us.'[14] She was insistent that she had become a murderer under this pressure which suggests that she had not merely discovered an exception to the prohibition on murder. It is this sort of understanding that Walzer wants to respect.

In discussion of this issue (after the lecture on which this chapter is based) Frances Kamm suggested that Walzer's position, or something like it, might be better understood if we invoked a distinction between acting wrongly and wronging someone. The agent who acts with dirty

[13] Thomas Nagel discusses something quite close to this sort of 'balanced exceptionism' in his paper 'War and Massacre' in *Mortal Questions* (Cambridge: Cambridge University Press, 1979), 62. He calls his version 'threshold deontology' as I noted earlier and contrasts it both with utilitarianism and absolutism.

[14] Quoted in Rab Bennett, *Under the Shadow of the Swastika: The Moral Dilemmas of Resistance and Collaboration in Hitler's Germany* (London: MacMillan, 1999), 291.

hands has not acted wrongly, he or she has done the right thing in the circumstances, but nonetheless the victim of the act has been wronged. As I recall, she gave the example of the bomber pilot who acts rightly in bombing an enemy munitions factory even though it is certain that the bombing will kill a small number of innocent non-combatants. Kamm thinks that the non-combatants were wronged by the right action and this is shown by the fact that they would be entitled to shoot and destroy the bomber before it could unload its bombs were they aware of the consequences for them. Perhaps Kamm's distinction can do some relevant work in this area, but there seem to be several problems with it as an elucidation of dirty hands. One is that Walzer would hardly count the case of the bomber as one of dirty hands since he accepts the doctrine of double effect (DDE) and the example is meant to satisfy proportionality of effect. Hence, he would hardly want to treat it in the same fashion as the direct and intentional killing of non-combatants that figures in his supreme emergency scenario. In the Kamm story the bomber does not violate the deep moral prohibition on intentionally killing the innocent. Of course, Kamm is critical of the DDE and this may be one reason she thinks the non-combatants are wronged.[15] But if we accept that some incidental killing (collateral damage) is morally legitimate in a just war, either because of the DDE or for some other principled reason, it is then unclear (at least to me) how the non-combatants in the Kamm story have been wronged. They have not been done an injustice, though their deaths are a horrible and deeply regrettable outcome of what we are assuming to be right action. It would of course be psychologically understandable (to say the least) that if they had access to appropriate weapons they might shoot down the bomber. Such (as Hobbes insisted) is the force of the imperative of self-preservation. It might even be morally excusable since they may not know, or positively disbelieve, that the target is legitimate or their likely deaths proportionate.

Two other comments are needed on the structure of Walzer's position. The first is that his present view of the matter is more restrictive than his original view in his influential dirty hands paper but it is more permissive than the main burden of his supreme emergency argument in *Just and Unjust Wars*. It is more restrictive because in the original

---

[15] See Frances Kamm, 'The Doctrine of Triple Effect and Why a Rational Agent Need Not Intend the Means to His End', *Proceedings of the Aristotelian Society*, suppl. vol. 74 (2000), 21–39.

paper his argument seemed much closer to a utilitarianism of extremity with the extreme being nowhere near the limit later set by supreme emergency. The need for torture concerned only the prevention of the probable killing of hundreds of innocent people, not the destruction of whole peoples and/or their ways of life. Moreover, Walzer's other example in the original paper was of a good democratic politician bribing a corrupt ward boss to deliver him votes with the promise of improperly delivered school construction contracts. Here the moral violation is not as great as in the former case, but nor could the emergency be considered 'supreme' in any sense. On the other hand, the emergencies mostly envisaged in *Just and Unjust Wars* concern such disasters as genocide and enslavement and the focus is on the evils of the Nazi threat. Indeed, so focused is Walzer on Nazi extermination strategies, that he regards the possible victory of Japan as an ordinary disaster, falling far short of supreme emergency. I have argued elsewhere that this seriously underestimates the threat posed by the Japanese government's racist militarism. But for now let us ignore this. The relevant point is that in his latest version of the dirty hands story, Walzer has opted for the much weaker criterion of threats to 'ways of life' which the Japanese expansion certainly posed and which are posed by many wars of conquest.

My second comment is that Walzer's position on dirty hands has always stressed the political order as the locus for the exemptions granted by the theory, but there is a question whether the problem of dirty hands might not arise in any sphere of life. Walzer's latest view makes it very implausible that this could be so, since supreme emergency is couched in terms of the political community, but he sometimes speaks more generally of 'the moral community' and we might at least wonder whether a parent faced with the 'necessity' of killing an innocent person to save her family or even herself is not in the area of emergency ethics. Consider the case of escapees from a Nazi camp who are in danger of being caught. As their pursuers come near, they hide quietly, but one of them is a mother carrying a baby who is beginning to cry. Unless the mother suffocates the baby, the group will be found and very likely killed. This seems very close to a dirty hands situation, though it has nothing directly political about it. Nor was Olga Lengyel a political leader defending a community's way of life, she was a victim trying to save other victims by victimizing further innocents. In both of these examples, however, it is a significant fact that the newborn child is almost certainly doomed to death at the hands of the Nazi authorities, and this is not an aspect of the political dirty hands scenarios that Walzer principally deals with.[16] Since my focus in this book is on political morality, I shall continue to follow Walzer in treating the dirty hands thesis as making a distinctive claim about politics.

ASSESSING THE DIRTY HANDS

So much for clarifying the theory of dirty hands, what about its truth? The most fundamental way to criticize the theory is to defend the overriding validity of the absolutist view of the impermissibility of torture or of the deliberate killing of the unconsenting innocent. There are at least three problems with this, however. The first (for me) is that I'm attracted to a modest version of such absolutism, but not sure I finally support it, partly because of the second problem, namely, that absolutism is obscure in many ways that need clearing up. These include the role and acceptability of the doctrine of double effect or some related principle, and the fact that every moral system has at least one absolute principle (for utilitarianism the dominance of maximizing happiness or preference satisfaction). I don't have the space here to pursue these matters, though I have said something about them elsewhere.[17] The third is that, despite the ubiquity of some absolutism at some level in every moral theory, the intellectual climate is so unsympathetic to more specific forms of absolutism, prohibiting particular types of wrongdoing rather than enjoining some foundational maxim, that attempts to defend it are likely to provoke peremptory dismissal. So, instead, I propose to explore the implications of the dirty hands doctrine against the background of the belief that the prohibitions on intentionally killing the innocent, on torture, and on slavery are now so deeply entrenched in our ways of thinking about morality that only an overwhelming case should make us consider violating them, and that even legitimate violations may have profound effects on our moral outlook. This puts me on common ground with Walzer who says in his latest attempt at the topic: 'I suggest a certain wariness about the

---

[16] Actually, although his original paper is significantly titled 'Political Action: the Problem of Dirty Hands', Walzer does admit at one point the possibility that hands might need to get dirty in non-political contexts (at p. 174.)

[17] See my ch. 14, 'The Issue of Stringency', in C. A. J. Coady, *Morality and Political Violence* (New York: Cambridge University Press, 2008).

exercise. As hard cases make bad law, so supreme emergencies put morality at risk. We need to be careful.'[18]

I want to urge several reasons for being careful, but first I want to challenge Walzer's communitarian defence of supreme emergency. Walzer denies that he is making 'a fetish of the political community' but that seems to me a pretty close description of what he does. The values of political community are indeed important—the good and central values, that is—but Walzer makes the idea of a coercive change to the expression of those values a supreme disaster in a fashion that is surely unacceptable. Most of the military conquests in history have involved such coercive changes at many levels, some more dramatic than others. The imposition of an alien state religion or political regime upon the conquered, even where it allows some minimal level of toleration, seems to fit Walzer's description and yet the need for prevention of this would make attacks upon the innocent and torture more routinely legitimate than he intends (assuming that such violations were likely to be successful). Cultural values are also more resilient than Walzer's argument allows. The totalitarian conquest and subsequent domination of Eastern Europe by the Soviet Union was a dreadful thing, but the communal life and values of Poland, Hungary, and so on survived, even though damaged in various ways. Had it been possible to prevent the conquest and domination by slaughtering hundreds of thousands of non-combatant Soviet citizens in the name of cultural preservation, would this have been a legitimate use of supreme emergency? The Princeton political theorist George Kateb once said to me in an aside when faced by an argument for war based on preserving community values: 'What, kill for a cuisine?' The ironic comment no doubt trivializes the values that communitarians are exalting, but it has a point. Community ties are important to our identities in various ways, but we need to be shown how 'identities' thus shaped can be so vital as to justify such horrors as terror bombing. It is, in addition, a puzzle that I have pointed to elsewhere that Walzer in a separate discussion of terrorism has categorically denied the benefits of supreme emergency to all non-state groups such as the Palestinians when they can mount a plausible case for the systematic destruction of their community life.[19] Significantly, however, in reprinting that essay on terrorism in a recent volume *Arguing About War*, he has added a bracketed

---

[18] Walzer, 'Emergency Ethics', 33.
[19] Walzer, 'Terrorism: A Critique of Excuses', ch. 4 in *Arguing About War*.

paragraph that partially acknowledges the problems posed by any such asymmetry between states and sub-state political groups. He now says (against the grain of the rest of his discussion) that considerations of supreme emergency may also apply to sub-state terrorists, 'but only if the oppression to which the terrorists claimed to be responding was genocidal in character' and he construes this as involving 'an imminent threat of political and physical extinction'.[20] He then claims that this has not been true of any recent terrorist cause.

We cannot pursue the defects of communitarianism further here so I will turn to other reasons for caution about the dirty hands exemptions. I would urge three reasons for being careful, indeed more careful than Walzer and other advocates of the doctrine are. The first is the danger of abuse. The second is the problem of static concentration on the dirty hands deed without attention to the dynamics of the situation that gives rise to its necessity. The third is the problem of corruption.

As for abuse, the supreme emergency story needs close attention to its primary factual premises. These are that the extreme circumstances (let's call them disaster circumstances) are imminent and that the grave violation is necessary or highly likely to avert them. It is not enough to produce philosophers' imaginary examples and then pretend that they apply in the real world. In his discussion of the very real Allied terror bombing of German cities in World War II, Walzer urges that the intentional killing of German civilians in 1940 and 1941 was a case of necessary dirty hands because it was the 'only option' available to the British at that time in the face of the imminent disaster of a German victory. Later it was, he argues, just morally criminal since the tide of the war had turned. But he also admits that the early bombing probably had very little impact on the course of the war. Moreover, there is considerable evidence that the British government knew, or could have known, at that early time that these deliberate massive killings of non-combatants would be ineffective. I have presented the evidence on this elsewhere and will not develop it here, but, if I am right, then this shows that one of the prime real life examples for the operation of dirty hands is defective. It is also significant that the 'ticking bomb' scenario that is invoked by theorists to justify torture is a highly idealized story that has little relation to real life. The story has it that the 'authorities' *know* that a bomb is set to go off and do massive damage, they *know* that the captive they have in custody *knows* the whereabouts of the

[20] Walzer, 'Terrorism: A Critique of Excuses', 54.

bomb and that torture is an efficient way to get the information from him or her, and that with the information they are very likely to be able to defuse the bomb and save innocent lives. In fact, the patchy record of intelligence services around the world should alert us to the disutility of these informational elements in the ticking bomb story. This record has been dramatically on view during the Iraq episode, but it has a long history. And the problem remains even if we replace knowledge with reasonable belief, though we do not want to lower the standard too much if we are concerned with the horrible degradation and suffering that is torture.

A further aspect of the factual realities of 'supreme emergency' is the way in which the conditions for resort to supreme emergency are liable to be subject to expansion and exploitation. Walzer's own example of the World War II bombing illustrates the point because the cry of 'supreme emergency' (the phrase was first coined by Churchill to justify the violation of the neutrality of Norway) not only was made to fit the terror bombing in the early, desperate phases of the war, but these bombings then inevitably continued on to the dreadful bombings of Hamburg and Dresden and so many other German cities, setting the moral climate for the fire-bombing of the Japanese mainland and the atomic bombings of Hiroshima and Nagasaki. Moreover, if supreme emergency exemptions are to be made part of the public regulation of moral and legal conduct in politics, particularly in war, then we should not be deluded into thinking that only 'the good guys' will have recourse to them.

My second point concerns the dangers in conceiving of the dirty hands problem in too static a way, as though the background circumstances in which hands are likely to get dirty are somehow immutable. Machiavellian thinking has a tendency to obscure the fact that the background to political life is itself a fit subject for moral scrutiny and structural change, especially when it is that background itself that contributes to the alleged need for dirty hands. Talk of the necessity for hands to get dirty often assumes a complacent, even conniving, tone, and tends to stifle the moral imagination, making local necessities seem global and eternal. This diverts attention from the many possibilities for structural, especially institutional, changes that might avoid the necessity for dirty hands. To take a common example: it is often argued that lying is endemic to democratic politics, not only in the sense that a lot of it goes on, but in the sense that a lot of it is sadly justifiable. Yet, the public is usually scornful of it and cynical about politicians' motives. Little attention is given to the need to develop practices and conventions that would reduce the temptations or necessities to lie. For instance, in the days of fixed exchange rates, the relevant politicians felt obliged to lie if questioned in parliament or press about a decision they had already taken to devalue. If a convention were in place that any such questions would never be answered, the necessity to lie would be removed, as it has been in many democracies where it is a convention that governments do not comment on certain questions about security matters. Such a convention may of course give rise to other moral and political problems, but it indicates one way that some 'necessary' immoralities (like lying) may be forestalled. Similarly with more serious immoralities—if you are in the sort of mess where it is necessary to violate a deep moral constraint then one important lesson may be to ensure that you (and others) don't get into such messes again. The Machiavellian outlook also puts morality into too defensive a posture, as though morality could only confront politics as an inhibition and a problem. But, although there are plenty of difficulties with a merely moralistic approach to politics, we must not lose sight of the power of morality as a dynamic for political change. The mostly peaceful overthrow of entrenched Communist tyranny in Eastern Europe, with all its ambiguities, is a timely reminder of this.[21]

Thirdly, there is the issue of corruption. Walzer wants the political leader to be a good man who must violate the deep moral constraints. We have seen that he is ambiguous about how this violation should be described, and I think that some of this ambiguity is related to the question of how persistent such violations must be. It may be that the occasional ghastly act of killing or torture can be vindicated as morally right and the agent's good character preserved. But it is naïve to think that dirty hands can be contained so easily. The political leader who ventures once on the path of torture in a good cause will very likely see more occasions for this resort, indeed will probably create more occasions by his initial act. He will then need trained torturers, manuals for torture, medical support staff to ensure the agony is delivered in such a way that the victim can survive to give information, smokescreen devices for keeping the facts from the public, and so on. So it is likely that such ramified violations would become a regular part of the political leader's vocation, as Weber seemed to believe.

---

[21] See Onora O'Neill, 'Politics, Morality, and the Revolutions of 1989', *Proceedings of the Aristotelian Society*, suppl. vol. 64 (1990), 281–94, in a symposium on Messy Morality and the Art of the Possible with C. A. J. Coady.

For Weber, in a violent world, the political leader's character had to be sacrificed to the public good. Endorsing Machiavelli's praise of those citizens who 'deemed the greatness of their native city higher than the salvation of their souls', Weber commented: 'He who seeks the salvation of the soul, of his own and of others, should not seek it along the avenue of politics, for the quite different tasks of politics can only be solved by violence.'[22] Ignoring the implicit claim that the use of violence must always be soul damning, we might see a link here with the dictum of Robert McNamara and question whether wholehearted engagement in evil or violation of the deep moral constraints in a good cause is essentially corrupting, and if so does it matter?

THE PROBLEM OF CORRUPTION

Corruption is an interesting concept and one relatively unexplored philosophically. Often our interest in corruption is the narrow one of financial corruption, but I am concerned here with the more general idea of moral corruption, and especially its manifestation in what is sometimes called 'noble corruption'. Let me begin with a general definition of corruption from which more specific types of corruption may be derived.

> Corruption is a condition of individuals, groups, or institutions that is characterized by immoral acts and activities, and an abiding tendency towards them, where these acts and activities substantially debase, distort, or destroy the morally appropriate operation of those individuals, groups, or institutions.

Much of the public corruption that is the stuff of media headlines can then be defined as occurring when public role bearers and those who deal with them in their public capacity deviate (in the manner specified in the general definition) from the morally legitimate responsibilities and duties inherent in that public office in order to secure a private benefit. Another form of public corruption that is of more philosophical interest is that sometimes referred to as noble or noble cause corruption, which differs from the standard public corruption only in the fact that its motivation is not private benefit but the desire to promote some perceived public good or to prevent some perceived public evil.[23]

---

[22] Weber, 'Politics as Vocation', 127.
[23] The term 'noble cause corruption' has a good deal of currency in writings about police ethics where it describes the corrupt practices of police seeking convictions, by

There is an initial puzzle about why we should be concerned with corruption at all. This is not to question the significance of those acts we call corrupt, such as receiving bribes, or contriving to appoint one's lover to a position of influence that he/she does not deserve, torturing prisoners of war or captives, or rigging an election. It is rather to puzzle over the need to be concerned with the disposition of mind that is said to be associated with these acts and to give rise to them. Surely, it is enough to condemn the acts, however they have arisen, and take steps to prevent such acts occurring? Yet when we are concerned with corruption we seem as concerned with the wrongful state of the individual or institution that has committed the acts complained of as with the acts themselves. This is reflected in the definitions given above. In the case of individuals, the dispositional state of mind that has given rise to the condemned acts seems a particular focus of our interest. Yet, as we shall see, there are some who argue that a concern with the corruption of mind, character, or soul is either incoherent or unimportant in the absence of the wrongful acts that such corruption might normally produce.

Let us explore this in more detail by examining some of the arguments in the debate over nuclear deterrence. Walzer was a participant in that debate and applied the idea of supreme emergency (and so, dirty hands) to offer a qualified defence of deterrence. This debate preoccupied many philosophers from, roughly, the 1960s until the end of the Cold War, but it is not merely historical in interest since deterrence theory is still at work in connection with both nuclear and chemical/biological weapons. The drive towards acquiring so-called Weapons of Mass Destruction (WMD) amongst so many middle powers and emerging players on the international scene derives partly from the allure of deterrence thinking. This is a fact often ignored by the established WMD powers who keep insisting that others not join the club. One reason why Israel, Pakistan, India, and China have nuclear weapons is that they have bought the argument that it is politically and morally necessary to defend themselves by deterrence (and possible use) of the power these weapons are supposed to give them. There is, for instance, much puzzlement in 'the West' about Saddam Hussein's continued failure

---

lying, planting false evidence, or torturing suspects, where they do so in order to protect the public. See e.g. Seumas Miller, 'Noble Cause Corruption in Policing', *African Security Review*, 8/3 (1999), 12–23, and Andrew Alexandra, 'Dirty Harry and Dirty Hands', in C. A. J Coady, Seumas Miller, Steve James, and Michael O'Keefe (eds.), *Violence and Police Culture* (Melbourne: Melbourne University Press, 2000), 235–48.

to dispel the widespread belief that he had substantial WMD capacity in the period leading up to the American-led invasion of his country. As it happened, Saddam's stance proved a disastrous miscalculation, but it is not really surprising that he adopted it, since it was perfectly consistent with the assumptions underlying deterrence theory. Faced with malevolent external threat, nations have invested in the possession of ghastly weapons partly in the belief that they provide insurance against an enemy attack. According to deterrence thinking, even the belief that you have such retaliatory capacity should provide a strong disincentive against attack. In Saddam's case there were various reasons why this idea should have been less impressive than he must have thought, including the fact that his supposed weapons couldn't have been delivered against the United States anyway, but deterrence theory has, in any case, many inherent defects. I merely cite the Iraq example as an illustration of its continued importance.

In the debate about deterrence, one argument used was that the conditional intention embodied in nuclear deterrence involved personal and institutional corruption. The deterrers intend to slaughter hundreds of thousands of innocent people if the enemy state does certain things. Of course they hope that the murderous threat will prevent the enemy so acting and hence suffice to guarantee that the intention will never be carried out. But they stand ready to unleash nuclear (or other WMD) devastation if deterrence fails. So, whether or not the agents of deterrence get to use the weapons to commit murder against civilian populations, each of them has become (as Anthony Kenny once put it) someone with 'murder in his heart'.[24] Stanley Benn mounted the argument with explicit reference to corruption, claiming that the practice of deterrence does violence to the moral natures of those who harbour the murderous (conditional) intention, and by extension corrupts the society that supports it.[25]

Against this, moderate supporters of deterrence, or critics of it with a different approach, mounted several objections. One, reminiscent of the 'dirty hands' debate, admits the evil of corruption but sees it as morally or politically necessary in the deterrent situation so that it is a form of 'noble corruption' or at least 'necessary corruption'. A second objection claims that the allegation of corruption puts the cart before the horse;

[24] Anthony Kenny, *The Logic of Deterrence* (London: Firethorn Press, 1985), 56.
[25] S. I. Benn, 'Deterrence or Appeasement? or On Trying to be Rational about Nuclear War', *Journal of Applied Philosophy*, 1 (1984), 15.

if the deterrent intention is corrupting, that is because it is wrong, it is not wrong because it is corrupting. Here the idea seems to be that the criticism of corruption has no independent life, it is just a sort of shorthand for some other recognizable form of wrongdoing.

DOES CORRUPTION MATTER IN ITSELF?

In different places, David Lewis offers two forms of the 'good corruption' argument, one more dismissive than the other. The less dismissive one allows that the deterrer has a bad character in one respect (the corruption) but has a good character in another (the effort to avert the great evil that is apparently being deterred). Lewis then denies that we have any use for 'a simple, unified, summary judgment' on those who have corrupted themselves in a good cause. They can be, as he says, both 'great patriots' and 'fiends in human shape'; it is basically a question of separate judgements on separate aspects of the person at one time, or even on the whole person at different times.[26] According to Lewis, any unified verdict could only be required by a Last Judge in a Last Judgement were there to be any such agent and event. But this ignores the fact that it is not only the Last Judge but the First Judge who needs a more holistic perspective. In other words, agents need to think of themselves as moral beings deciding on a course of action in the light of what they will be or become in so acting. Agents need a sense of their own integrity and should aim ideally at moral coherence. I say 'ideally' because such integrity may not be fully realizable, just as rational coherence in thought or action is rarely, if ever, achievable. Nonetheless, they are goals to be (non-neurotically) pursued and such a striking discordance between the two ways of being, as described by Lewis, can hardly be tolerable to a moral agent. To illustrate his point, Lewis mentions the 'conscientious Nazi' discussed by Philippa Foot, but the example shows (to the contrary) that there *is* a need for an overall judgement.[27] The Nazi sees himself as, amongst other things, a good patriot and fails to see himself at all as a 'fiend in human shape' but were he to gain that insight he could hardly treat the relation between these

[26] David Lewis, 'Devil's Bargains in the Real World', in Douglas MacLean (ed.), *The Security Gamble: Deterrence Dilemmas in the Nuclear Age* (Totowa, NJ: Rowan and Allenheld, 1984), 144–5.
[27] Ibid. 145–6.

two aspects as casually as Lewis suggests. He needs the unified verdict in order to make sense of himself as a moral agent, and, if he needs it, so surely do we.

In a later essay, Lewis is more brisk with the corruption difficulty, dismissing any concern for the 'heart and soul' of the deterrer (or the just warrior more generally) as merely 'self-regarding'. As he puts it, 'other things at stake in warfare are just much more important than the state of the warrior's heart and soul'.[28] This echoes Gregory Kavka's discussions of the paradoxes of deterrence where Kavka argues for the moral legitimacy of 'self-corruption' in the pursuit of such overwhelming good as deterrence is supposed to deliver.[29] They both think it is morally right to form the conditional intention to slaughter the innocent, though it would be morally wrong to implement it. (Lewis in fact, at least at one stage, was convinced that the actual deterrence policies of the USA did not involve the suspect intention so that the paradox of deterrence was largely a philosopher's exercise.[30] I have argued elsewhere that he is wrong about this, but will not discuss it here.[31]) They both think that what Kavka calls 'the wrongful intention principle' (WIP) is plausible but mistaken as a generally valid principle.[32] The WIP says that: 'if it is wrong to do X, it is wrong to intend to do it'. Kavka and Lewis reject the principle because they think one can separate the forming of an intention to do X and the doing of X in such a way as to form separate judgements on the morality of each.

This light-hearted attitude to self-corruption seems to me deeply flawed both morally and philosophically. At the philosophical level it treats 'forming an intention' as an isolated act that bears a merely contingent connection to carrying the intention out, whereas the fact is that we could not treat someone as genuinely intending to do X unless they were thereby bent upon doing X, making arrangements to facilitate the bringing about of X and so on. The conditional deterrent intention, it is true, is supposed to have certain 'autonomous effects' (as Kavka puts it) that are not only good, but believed to make it less likely that

---

[28] See 'Finite Counterforce', in Henry Shue (ed.), *Nuclear Deterrence and Moral Restraint* (New York: Cambridge University Press, 1989), 95.

[29] See Gregory Kavka, 'Some Paradoxes of Deterrence', *Journal of Philosophy*, 75/6 (1978), 295–8.

[30] Lewis, 'Devil's Bargains in the Real World', 146–51.

[31] See C. A. J. Coady, 'Escaping from the Bomb', in Shue (ed.), *Nuclear Deterrence and Moral Restraint*, 180–3.

[32] Kavka, 'Some Paradoxes of Deterrence', 289.

the intention will need to be implemented (by making the condition less likely to occur).[33] There are various reasons to doubt the truth of this latter belief, but I shall not discuss them here. What is clearly true is that your conditional intention makes it more likely that *you* will engage in nuclear war than if you had no such aims. This link between intention and outcome remains intact. Moreover, other far less welcome 'autonomous effects' of the deterrent posture are now becoming evident in the post-Cold War world of nuclear (and WMD) proliferation and the prospect of terrorist resort to such weapons.

These unwelcome effects are related to the corruption issue. Some stem from the perceptions that others are likely to have of the noble self-corruptors. Though the latter see themselves as acting from noble motives, they are likely to appear simply corrupt to much of the outside world. The corruption of the nuclear deterrers not only establishes a relation between what they intend and what they will do by way of nuclear war, but it also connects with their other intentions, beliefs, desires, and practical thinking in ways that amount to a damaging stance towards the world. That they are prepared to massacre millions, wreak massive destruction on the environment, and shatter the cultural and political heritage of future generations in pursuit of good or avoidance of evil (as they presently perceive these) requires them to think and act in terms of protecting the deterrent strategy and all it involves. So the corrupt mindset is not something protected from view by 'Cartesian privacy', it is essentially oriented towards public action, even in the special case of the deterrent posture, and this orientation has implications for behaviour beyond the deterrence context. This complex of facts will in turn influence the reactions of outsiders who need to know what type of person(s) they are dealing with. Lewis's attempt to make the concern with corruption seem a matter of spiritual navel-gazing ignores all of this. The concern for character is a concern for morally healthy or unhealthy dispositions to action so when we worry about the corrupt character of an individual or institution or society we are not concerned with something simply introspective and irrelevant to public good.

The other objection mentioned earlier about the cart before the horse contains similar confusions. It was urged in the nuclear deterrence debate by Jeff McMahan who claimed that if the intention to do what is wrong (as in the deterrence strategy) is corrupting, that is because

---

[33] Kavka, 'Some Paradoxes of Deterrence', 291.

it is wrong, it is not wrong because it is corrupting.[34] Now, it is true that the wrongness of some intention must derive from the wrongness of the act upon which it is directed, but this does not mean that there is no point in characterizing the agent's state in having the intention as corrupt. As we noted in the earlier analysis of the idea of corruption, someone's engaging in a single act of wrongdoing does not make the person thereby corrupt. And similarly, an agent's setting themselves to do some wrong will be wrong, even if they don't get to do it, but this sole wrongful intention may not mean that they are corrupt. The corruption of nuclear deterrence is not that of a single lapse into evil, but of a sustained, bolstered, ramified orientation. In McNamara's phrase quoted earlier it is an engagement *in* evil. Similarly with other forms of corruption. McMahan's objection could however be read as rejecting the idea that the dirty hands deterrer is doing wrong in any sense at all, and so is not involved in corruption since there is no deviation from the morality of her public office. Whether this is consistent with the admission that deterrence is an instance of dirty hands will depend on which way one goes on the structural issues discussed in section 1.

I have been trying to show that the case for 'necessary corruption' or 'good corruption' is much harder to make than its supporters think. And this has implications well beyond the nuclear deterrence debate. It is relevant, for instance, to debates about torture, grave suspensions of civil liberties, and policies towards asylum seekers, to name just a few issues of public concern. But two things may be objected at this point. One is that I haven't shown that the evil of self-corruption may not sometimes be outweighed by any good effects it might have. The other is that my case rests too much on an undifferentiated view of character; it suggests that bad character in one area must infect the whole personality or soul, and this goes against the known facts of compartmentalization.

Here I shall have to be brief, certainly briefer than the issues warrant. On the first point, I doubt that it is possible to present a global argument to such a conclusion and I have principally been arguing for the weaker conclusion that most arguments for good corruption, especially self-corruption in a good cause, underestimate the task they face. Indeed, I do *not* want to argue that the good effects of corruption can never lead to the overall verdict that in some particular context, corruption is a good thing. It is surely sensible to describe as a good thing overall the

---

[34] Jeff McMahan, 'Deterrence and Deontology', *Ethics*, 95/3 (Apr. 1985), 523.

existence of corrupt public officials in an evil regime who take bribes to allow persecuted groups facing torture and death to escape the regime. These good effects of the corruption outweigh (or can outweigh) the bad effects of having corrupt public officials, especially where the institutions those officials serve have goals that are already distorted by the evil of the regime. Indeed, if the officials were not helping the victims to escape for motives of greed, they would be promoting immoral persecution for the sake of rectitude in their role where this rectitude is twisted to the service of evil ends. This judgement seems secure even though there are tricky philosophical questions lurking around it, like what account of the virtues are we to give when it is better for agents of an evil regime to have certain vices rather than the corresponding virtues.

On the second point, I would not want to deny the human capacity to shut off areas of psychic life to the influence of other areas. I have argued only that corruption is a dispositional state of mind pointing in two directions: one aimed at public actions and the other at collateral mental states. You cannot be corruptly seeking bribes unless you are on the lookout for opportunities for fulfilling your intentions, thinking about ways to disguise your intentions from certain people and to enlist others in the operation where appropriate, and so on. This does not mean that your state of character must lead you to extract bribes from your family and friends, or develop tendencies to wrongdoing of quite different sorts. No corruption thesis should, or need, be as strong as this. On the other hand, compartmentalization is probably a more volatile and ambiguous phenomenon than it is often made to seem. Men who have endured the horrors of war and often have done hideous things that they would never countenance in peacetime will often return to civilian life apparently unaffected by their experiences. Yet, it has become increasingly clear in recent years that an apparent calm can conceal deep trauma. Post-traumatic stress can affect many areas of the personality and it is real enough even if theoretical accounts of it are currently not wholly satisfactory. This suggests that the attempt to shut off areas of psychological disposition from the effects of corruption is not as straightforward as it might appear.

FINAL OBJECTION

The most radical criticism of the corruption story comes in the wake of a drastic objection to the very existence of character and character traits. If there are no character traits, there is no character and no virtue or vice. If this were so, then the corruption story, as I have told it, would at least lose much of its point since it is a story about settled dispositions to behave badly. I haven't cast my version directly in terms of virtues and vices, but it is a story about the morally distorted character of individuals, groups, and institutions and hence it would seem to be vulnerable to this radical critique.

The 'eliminativist' critique of character has been strongly urged by Gil Harman in a series of recent papers.[35] He argues that just as we have many entrenched common-sense views about the physical world that have been shown to be false by physical science, so too have our common-sense (and philosophical) views about character traits been destroyed by social science. In particular, the work of various social psychologists is supposed to offer support for the eliminativist thesis. It does this principally by exhibiting the way in which our beliefs in character etc. exhibit 'the fundamental attribution error' (hereafter FAE). What is this error?

It is, I think, hard to get clear about the exact nature of FAE, from the various expositions Harman gives or cites, but it seems to consist in mistakenly explaining a person's performance in terms of a character attribute 'rather than' details of the situation in which he or she acts.[36] The sort of thing Harman means can be gathered from the psychological studies that he cites, principally the Milgram experiments on obedience to authority and the Darley/Batson 'Good Samaritan' experiment. Here, I have space to consider only the latter. This is the well-known experiment with students at the Princeton Theological Seminary, who were assigned to give talks on various subjects at a building some distance away. Along the path they had to walk past an actor pretending to be in distress. The psychologists were testing the conditions under which the students would stop to help, so some students were told they were late and should hurry, others that they just had enough time, and others that they had plenty of time. Some students were assigned the parable of the Good Samaritan as the topic for their talk, others were given quite different topics. According to a

---

[35] 'Moral Philosophy Meets Social Psychology: Virtue Ethics and the Fundamental Attribution Error', *Proceedings of the Aristotelian Society*, 99 (1999), 315–31; 'The Nonexistence of Character Traits', *Proceedings of the Aristotelian Society*, 100 (2000), 223–6; 'No Character or Personality', *Business Ethics Quarterly*, 13/1 (Jan. 2003), 87–94.

[36] Harman, 'Moral Philosophy Meets Social Psychology', 322–4.

questionnaire administered earlier, the students had a variety of moral and religious outlooks.

Famously, the highest percentage of those who stopped to help were in the group that believed they didn't have to hurry (63 per cent), next were those in a moderate hurry (45 per cent), and only 10 per cent of those in a great hurry stopped to help. The topics of their talk had no influence on behaviour nor did their moral and religious outlook. The outcome is both amusing and a little depressing. But what does it show about character traits?

Harman thinks that it shows that we are wrong to explain the surprisingly 'bad behaviour' of the non-helpers by resort to ideas about their bad character such as 'callousness'. Similarly, we are wrong to look for an explanation of the difference between the helpers and the non-helpers in terms of dispositional character traits 'rather than' in situational factors such as the hurry factor.

There is no doubt that the situation in which agents find themselves makes a powerful contribution to how they will react to it. We hardly need psychologists to prove that, though their work may reveal surprising facts about how influential certain situational factors can be. It is, however, a further, huge step to make the stark contrast that Harman and the FAE provide between the broadly dispositional and the situational elements. Calling for attention to aspects of the situation *instead* of dispositions of the agent is absurd because we need to invoke dispositions of the agent in order to explain why the situational factors work. Dispositions towards punctuality, towards success in work, towards obedience are some of those needed to make sense of these experimental outcomes. Indeed, even some of the much-maligned character traits such as callousness, selfishness, insensitivity, or contempt for the unfortunate may be required to account for the usually ignored but remarkable fact that 37 per cent of the students who were *not* in a hurry failed to stop and help the victim.

More generally there is clearly something self-defeating in any interpretation of the FAE that makes it prove that we are wrong to look for explanations of behaviour in broad dispositions of the agent 'rather than' elements of the situation, since the FAE itself offers just such an explanation of the failings of common sense.[37] Harman is aware

---

[37] This defect has been remarked by both Owen Flanagan and David Coady in separate discussions. See David Coady, 'Conspiracy Theories and Official Stories', in David Coady (ed.), *Conspiracy Theories: The Philosophical Debate* (Aldershot: Ashgate,

of this general problem and has a sort of response to it. He says, 'To deny that people differ significantly in character traits is not to deny that they have any dispositions at all'.[38] It is only character traits that are undermined by the FAE. So people can share broad dispositional personality traits conceived of as habitual tendencies to act in a certain fashion such as those involved in the FAE and the confirmation bias (tendency to see only evidence that supports one's hypothesis and ignore contradictory evidence) as well as personality disorders and mental illness. But if people can have these, why not character traits? Perhaps, the thesis here is that the experiment shows that they just don't. But the Good Samaritan experiment neither shows nor tends to show anything of the sort. It may suggest that the attribution of character traits should proceed more cautiously than it sometimes does. A comment by one psychologist seems to be making this point. Kunda (quoted by Harman) says:

The librarian carried the old woman's groceries across the street. The receptionist stepped in front of the old man in line. The plumber slipped an extra $50 into his wife's purse. Although you were not asked to make any inferences about any of these characters, chances are that you inferred that the librarian is helpful, the receptionist rude, and the plumber generous. Perhaps because we do not realise the extent to which behaviour is shaped by situations, we tend to spontaneously infer such traits from behaviour.[39]

In the absence of fuller description or more complete understanding of some situation we might well make a misjudgement of character but this does nothing to show that we will persist in the mistake when fuller information comes to hand. Nor, of course, does it undermine our capacity to get it right when information is available. If we find that the plumber is using his wife to spread counterfeit notes we will have no tendency to call him 'generous' on the basis of this action. (Contrary to Harman's claim that we have a strong tendency to stick to our initial attributions of character 'in the face of considerable disconfirming evidence'.)[40] And parallel amendments to the other briefly described events would surely evoke equally rapid adjustments. So, these cases don't even show that people are incautious in their character attributions.

2006), 124–5, and Owen Flanagan, *Varieties of Moral Personality: Ethics and Psychological Realism* (Cambridge, Mass.: Harvard University Press, 1991), 305.

[38] Harman, 'Moral Philosophy Meets Social Psychology', 327.
[39] Harman, 'No Character or Personality', 89.   [40] Ibid. 90.

More generally, it is no intrinsic part of character discourse that it should be crude and unsubtle or insensitive to context. Nor is it part of character attributions that people cannot act out of character or reform or destroy their characters. In so far as talk of corruption is part of character discourse the same points apply.

In conclusion, let me return to the Ignatieff article I cited at the beginning. There is a curious phenomenon often associated with the dirty hands debate that is exemplified in his article. It is a combination of a high-minded naïvety about present realities and a descent into murky advocacy of the necessity of adopting dirty tactics in the future. Ignatieff spends a good deal of his article arguing that it is time to abandon American moral and legal reticence about assassination without showing any awareness that official US qualms about assassination are largely rhetorical. US agencies have seldom hesitated to support assassination or its close relatives, as the demise of Lamumba and Allende illustrates dramatically, and Castro's survival is a testament to the incompetence of those agencies rather than their moral restraint. And these are only the high-profile cases; there are many more cases of assassinations, sponsored or approved by US agencies in areas such as South America. True, the US officially disapproves of Israel's policy of extensive resort to targeted assassination, but, to say the least, it puts no serious pressure on the Israelis to stop it. And quite apart from assassination, the US authorities have been engaged for over fifty years at least in numerous illegal and immoral undercover operations to destabilize and overthrow governments, often democratically elected, that the US government of the day, or its agents, disliked. Subversion of foreign governments, massive deception at home and abroad, sustaining vicious dictatorships in programmes of terrorism, all this has been a staple of standard operations, not rare resorts in supreme emergency. As for torture, Ignatieff decides against it after much heart-searching, but shows no awareness that United States agencies have been involved in torture for decades. The infamous School of the Americas (SOA, now called the Western Hemisphere Institute for Security Co-operation) in Fort Benning, Georgia, trained torturers to ply their trade in Central and South America and a commitment to torture at senior military and governmental levels has been apparent in the recent revelations from Iraq. The Pentagon was forced to admit in 1996 that the SOA had training manuals with instructions in torture as well as in 'neutralizing' (i.e., killing). These were not only used in courses at the School but printed in Spanish and distributed in appropriate places in Latin America.[41] There is something paradoxical about high-minded intellectuals urging their governments to be less morally squeamish when the same governments are already up to their armpits in dirt. If our rulers were behaving like Erasmus' Christian Prince who was portrayed as an exemplar of Christian virtue, there *might* be some point in urging a more relaxed attitude to high moral standards, but where their actual practice, as opposed to their sentimental rhetoric, is so thoroughly sleazy and 'engaged in evil', the defence and advocacy of dirty hands will inevitably court the dangers of bad faith.

[41] See Dana Priest, 'U.S. Instructed Latins On Executions, Torture; Manuals Used 1982–91, Pentagon Reveals', *Washington Post* (21 Sept. 1996), and Steven Lee Myers, 'Old U.S. Army Manuals for Latin Officers Urged Rights Abuses', *New York Times* (22 Sept. 1996). See also Alfred W. McCoy, *A Question of Torture: C. I. A. Interrogation from the Cold War to the War on Terror* (New York: Henry Holt & Company, 2006).

5
Politics and Lying

> To know how to dissemble is the knowledge of kings.
> Cardinal Richelieu, *Mirame*

Dishonesty has always been perceived in our culture, and in all cultures but the most bizarre, as a significant human vice. Moreover, the specific form of dishonesty known as lying has generally been scorned, and the habitual liar treated with contempt. Hence, the accusation of lying is a potent tool in politics, as Tony Blair and George Bush have been discovering to their cost, because exposure of their deceptive conduct over Iraq, frequently characterized as lying, seemed part of the cause of their electoral unpopularity. There are perfectly good reasons for the common hostility to lying that I will shortly explore, but we should note at the outset that this perception is consistent with a certain hesitancy about what constitutes a lie and with the more than sneaking suspicion that there might be a number of contexts in which lying is actually justified, and others in which it is at least excusable. There is also the important fact that obfuscating, deliberately misleading, and evading are forms of deceit that can often be just as morally questionable as lying and sometimes more effective. In the context of politics, there is a long tradition of rulers deceiving the ruled, and contemporary cynicism about democratic politicians is such that their mendacity is almost taken for granted and hence, though seldom regarded as justified, often has less damaging political consequences for them than might be expected. So it is that the former Australian Prime Minister, John Howard, maintained significant popular support even though opinion polls consistently reported that he is widely believed to have lied or countenanced lies about the 'children overboard' affair and the justifications for Australia's participation in the Iraq war.[1] Howard has subsequently been defeated at the 2007 election and it is possible that his reputation for playing fast and loose with the facts contributed to his crushing defeat (he not only lost government but also his own seat) yet other factors, such as disastrous industrial relations legislation, seem to have been more significant.

Complexity in attitudes to political lying can be found at the very beginning of our intellectual tradition where we find the genius of Plato deployed in defence of the politically expedient lie. In the first great Western work of political theory, *The Republic*, Plato defends the idea that rulers should lie to their citizens where it is for the citizens' benefit, and this follows naturally from his claim that the rulers themselves should be deceived, if possible, by a 'noble lie' about their origins.[2] The different classes of society were to be made to believe that they were fashioned differently by God (the rulers having a quantity of gold in their make-up where farmers and craftsmen had only iron and brass) so that they would more readily accept their roles.

Subsequent philosophical tradition has vacillated between Plato's bold paternalism and a total rejection of lying. St Augustine and Immanuel Kant condemned lying in any circumstances, though Augustine thought some lies much graver than others. By contrast, the nineteenth-century moral philosopher Henry Sidgwick thought that the public might have to be deceived about the very nature of morality. Sidgwick thought that a certain version of utilitarianism was the real truth about how we should live, but also thought that if the world at large knew and acted upon the principle of utility then the results would be disastrous. His idea was that if everyone acted with an exclusive eye to the utilitarian principle of doing only what contributed to the greatest happiness of the greatest number (rather than acting in accord with established moral rules and principles) the inevitable miscalculations, misunderstandings, and destruction of trust would lead to widespread misery and institutional breakdown. So utilitarianism itself required that most people not act upon it. Only the elite few could be trusted to frame their actions on

---

[1] See Michael Gordon, 'PM Lied Over Children: Poll', *The Age*, Melbourne (8 Sept. 2004).

[2] See Plato, *The Republic*, 459c and 414d (any edn.).

the basis of seeking the greatest happiness of the greatest number, and their principles should be kept secret from the hoi polloi who could get on with ordinary duty and morality. If the price of such secrecy was that the elite had to lie to the masses then presumably so be it.[3] Sidgwick also thought it perfectly admissible to lie to children or the sick if you thought the truth would be injurious to them.[4] Interestingly, we are much less confident about these categories than Sidgwick and his contemporaries were, and that is partly because we are much more impressed with the value of autonomy and the associated right to have enough information to govern the direction of your own life even if you are very sick or very young.

Even some of those who thought it always wrong to lie were driven by the complex intricacies of life to acknowledge that there might be legitimate ways of speaking with intent to mislead that did not count as lies, and were sometimes morally defensible. The late medieval tradition of casuistry, so bitterly and sometimes unfairly attacked by Pascal, devoted much ingenuity, some of it certainly twisted, to the discussion of such matters under the heading of equivocation and mental reservation. These theorists were concerned with the interpretation of moral rules, especially in the context of the confessional, and kept a close eye on unusual or challenging circumstances in which it was difficult to determine what is right. Some of their focus was on what would often be called these days 'moral dilemmas'. Because of their interest in care for ordinary tempted mortals, the casuists developed a concern for the way in which moral rules and principles had to be adapted to the messy peculiarities of daily life. But to this I shall return.

DEFINING LIES

It is time to look to matters definitional. Lying is a species of dishonesty. Honesty involves more than veracity, but includes it. The honest man keeps faith broadly; his word is his bond and he doesn't lie. But what are lies? Why do they matter morally? And how strict is the prohibition against them?

---

[3] Henry Sidgwick, *The Methods of Ethics*, 7th edn. (London: Macmillan, 1963), 489–90.
[4] Ibid. 316.

Although theorists have differed strikingly on how to define a lie, there is a central core of agreement that a lie is at least the stating of what one believes to be false with the intention of giving an audience to understand that it is true. Let us call this the descriptive definition. For some, this is not a sufficient characterization because they think we do not lie if we speak thus to an audience which has no right, in the circumstances, to the truth. The sort of case that raises the question of a right to the truth most dramatically and also poses the most obvious and striking challenge to the absolutist about lying was anticipated by St Augustine. He asked in his treatise 'On Lying' whether it might be permissible to lie in order to avoid betraying 'a just and innocent man' (or even a guilty one) to capital punishment.[5] He answered firmly, though against his natural inclinations, that it was not. But others would say that the woman who tells the Nazi thugs that she has no Jews in the house though she knows she has a Jewish refugee in the cellar is not even lying because the Nazis have no right to this truth. They add to the descriptive definition the proviso that the audience must have a right to the truth.

This definitional strategy is not merely devised to avoid a difficulty. It is based on the thought that dishonesty is a form of injustice, and that what is wrong with it is its injuring of the rights of others to the truth. This is the line taken by the great Protestant philosopher, theologian, and jurist Hugo Grotius, one of the founders of the field of international law. Here is Grotius defending this approach: 'Then further, it is required that the right which is infringed belong to him with whom we converse, and not to another, just as in the case of contracts also injustice arises only from an infringement of the right of the contracting parties.'[6] And he goes on to insist that the wrong of lying resides in the injustice done to an intended audience.

One advantage of this sort of definition is that it may enable us to hold that lying is always wrong, because it excludes the most awkward cases of what seem to be good 'untruths' from the category of lies. It also has the consequence, drawn by Grotius and others, that an audience can waive its rights to the truth, and that, where it has, one does not lie to eavesdroppers for whom the communication is not intended.

---

[5] Augustine, 'Lying', in *Treatises on Various Subjects*, ed. Roy J. Deferrari (Washington, DC: Catholic University of America Press, 1965), 83.

[6] Hugo Grotius, *On the Law of War and Peace* (Oxford: Clarendon Press; London: Humphrey Milford, 1925), bk. 3, ch. 1, §11.2, p. 614.

Knowing, for instance, that your office phone is likely to be bugged by a rival corporation or by secret police, you explain to your family in advance that any business information you tell them on that phone may well be false. You then tell them about some non-existent deal and the business rivals are bugging the phone and are deceived, but not lied to. Certainly, the family is not lied to, having waived their right to such information (at least from you on the phone) and you are not addressing the eavesdroppers. One might, of course, say that you intended to deceive the eavesdroppers, but I am not sure that this is true of the case as described. Perhaps you have a conditional intention that if there is a surreptitious audience, they will be deceived, so your performance embodies a conditional lying. In any event, since they have no right to the truth in these circumstances, it will not be a lie (on a Grotian definition) even if you do intend to deceive them.

This approach will also mean that the woman does not lie to the Nazi thugs when she tells them that there is no Jew in her house. It is, I think, possible to operate with such a concept of lying, but it strikes me as inconsistent with our actual linguistic practices, for it seems counter-intuitive to hold that the woman hasn't lied to the Nazis. So I prefer to operate with the more descriptive definition of lying, which makes no reference to rights, and which then must face up to the question of exceptions. The issue of an audience's right to the truth, or lack of it, will then come up as a central moral issue determining the wrong of lying and possibly when it is permissible to lie.

What the speaker believes is all-important, and, in the case of some people in public life, part of our problem seems to be that they have trouble knowing what that is at any given time. The intent to deceive is a crucial element of the definition because we do not want to say that many jokes or literary pretences which involve falsehood are lies, or that uttering false statements in the course of testing someone's hearing are lies. Of course, some jokes are intended to deceive, albeit briefly, and much Christian tradition, especially that influenced by Augustine, has classified them as lies and frowned upon them, whilst treating them as less sinful than many other categories of lie. But neither is all deception lying; deception is a broader category than lying and may sometimes be justified where lying is not. I cannot be obliged to make sure that everyone has true beliefs so I may very well be entitled to remain silent about the truth when it is clear that someone who might expect me to correct them is in error. Furthermore, it is possible to deceive someone by telling them the truth for you may know they will make a false inference from your truth-telling. You may even be able to take advantage of the fact that some audience does not trust your word so that by telling the truth you may ensure that they conclude to what is false.

It is also important to remark that there are wrongful deceptions that do not quite count as lying, but belong, as it were, on the penumbra of the direct lie. These can include, for example, confident assertions that the speaker believes but on insufficient evidence, or even in the face of strong contrary evidence. Such assertions are vicious where the speaker has an obligation, perhaps because of his or her office, to refrain from such confident utterance where sufficiently strong evidence is lacking and they know it. They are not outright lies because the speaker believes what she says, but the claims deceive the audience about the strength of the support for the belief and are usually intended to do so. Some of Tony Blair's or Colin Powell's confident claims about Iraq's weapons of mass destruction seem to fall into this category. (For illustrative purposes, I am giving them the benefit of the doubt here about the sincerity of the belief their utterances expressed.) There are also cases where the speaker asserts p intending to get an audience to believe it while not being sure whether she herself believes it or not. Driven by the good that will be achieved if the audience believes p, a politician may assert it as a fact even when she only 'half-believes' it. President Bush's assertion in a State of the Union address that the British government had 'learned' that Saddam Hussein had recently sought significant quantities of uranium from Africa may fall into this or the previous category (if he was not simply lying) since these rumours had much earlier been found unreliable by the CIA. Bush and his supporters later tried to justify this speech by saying that the President spoke truthfully because British authorities had indeed made such a public claim. They had, but the CIA had already made it clear to the White House that the claim was probably false, so the President's use of it to bolster his case was deceitful, if not an outright lie. (Actually, whether it was a lie depends upon whether the use of 'learned' implies the truth of what has been so acquired.) I shall return to the moral importance of these sorts of deceptions later.

LEGITIMATE LIES AND MISLEADINGS?

Definition aside, there is the issue of morality. Lying is wrong because dishonesty is a vice. Communication is built upon an element of trust, and so is much else that is essential to our lives together. Liars trade upon and betray this trust, usually in pursuit of self-interest, and their activities debase the currency of language and undermine to some extent the ease of communal interactions. Even someone as sceptical as Montaigne condemns lying in terms as ferocious as Kant: 'Lying is an accursed vice. It is only our words which bind us together and make us human. If we realized the horror and weight of lying we would see that it is more worthy of the stake than other crimes . . . Once let the tongue acquire the habit of lying and it is astonishing how impossible it is to make it give it up.'[7] The debasement to which Montaigne points, though real, shouldn't however be exaggerated; communicative prospects do not collapse utterly in the face of a certain degree of lying, because we learn to discount for common areas of deceit and lying. So it is that we take the eulogies of used car salesmen and real estate agents with a touch of salt, and seldom trust fully most electoral promises. Nonetheless, a reputation for lying is a bad thing to have, and most people are quick to reject accusations of lying.

But is lying always morally wrong? As we have seen, some of the greatest thinkers in our tradition have thought that it is. St Augustine and Immanuel Kant are amongst the most unyielding rigorists on this matter. Kant declared that the duty not to lie was 'an unconditional duty which holds in all circumstances'.[8] Lying vitiates the source of all law and deforms the liar by destroying his human dignity and making him worse than a mere thing.

Yet so stern a position is hard to accept in several types of circumstance. Indeed, many Christian thinkers before Augustine had taught that lying was sometimes (though rarely) justified, and had pointed to instances of lying and dissembling in the Bible. The great Christian humanist Erasmus thought Augustine's rigorism impossible in practice, and fundamentally unrealistic. The circumstances that challenge the rigorist position embrace the extremes of triviality and disaster. Some lies are so removed from the context of harm and benefit that they seem morally insignificant. Someone who is embarrassed by another's effusive thanks for some kind act which cost quite a lot may nonetheless try to stop the flow of thanks by saying untruthfully, 'It was nothing really.' Or we may greet a tiresome acquaintance with 'How nice to see you' whilst

---

[7] Montaigne, *On Liars*, in *The Complete Essays of Michael de Montaigne*, ed. M. A. Screech (London: Allen Lane, 1991), 35.

[8] Immanuel Kant, 'On A Supposed Right to Lie from Altruistic Motives', in *Critique of Practical Reason and Other Writings in Moral Philosophy*, ed. Lewis White Beck (Chicago: University of Chicago Press, 1949), 349.

feeling nothing but distaste for the encounter. In other contexts, a lie may be required to preserve a pleasant surprise for the audience, as when you have organized a surprise birthday occasion for a workmate who announces unexpectedly that she is leaving work half an hour early (and that is half an hour before the surprise event). So, you tell her falsely that she is required to stay for some urgent business that has just come up. Some of these utterances, like 'how nice to see you', may not even be lies because the strength of custom or convention can attach to them in ways that eliminate their force as statements or override any intent to deceive.

This point about convention is interesting, because where people do not expect a speaker to tell the truth, for reasons unconnected with his honesty, then his saying what is false may not have the force of a lie and may even produce good or prevent evil. In the domain of modern politics, for instance, a Treasurer may be asked some direct question about a possible devaluation of the currency (in those now rare cases where a currency is not free-floating) in a context where refusal to answer will be taken as confirmation of a devaluation. She has, let us say, already decided to announce a devaluation the next week, but the economy will take an unnecessary battering if the word is out before then. Whatever she has decided, she is expected to say 'No', so the element of deception has almost disappeared. Cardinal Newman gives an interesting example, which he attributes to Burke, of someone making it clear in his utterance that it is not to be taken as a serious disavowal. The speaker has been asked for some information that he is not at liberty to reveal so he says: 'Whether I had done the thing or not, I would say to you that I had not done it. But let me say: "I did not do it." '[9]

At the other extreme, lying to save an innocent person or group from genuine disaster may be justified by those very requirements of virtue that ground the prohibition on lying itself. This is especially cogent when one lies to those who are malevolently bent upon inflicting the disaster (as in the Nazi example.) If we think, like Grotius, in terms of rights and injustice, then we can't help reflecting that we may be morally entitled to defend the life of the fugitive Jew by directing violence against the Nazi thug even to the point of bringing about his death. But if that is permissible, why is it forbidden to lie to him? Indeed, this is an

---

[9] I recall Newman as the source of this amusing anecdote but have been unable to locate the reference. I doubt Newman (or Burke!) would be unhappy with the attribution, even if it is mistaken.

instance of the more general puzzle: moralists like Augustine and Kant allow that it is sometimes permissible to kill perpetrators of injustice in a just cause, as in a just war, or a legitimate execution, but not permissible to lie to the unjust in a just cause.

This point prompts the reflection that if there can be just wars (as Augustine certainly allowed) then their successful prosecution seems to require a good deal of deception of the enemy, including, in some contexts, lying. There are of course dangers in lying to the enemy, since even considerations of utility make it clear that some degree of trust between enemies is necessary in war. So just war theorists and international lawyers have devoted considerable energy to putting some limits on deception of the enemy, including the proscription of the category of perfidy, but this is against the background of other legitimate deceptions, including lies. We might also reflect that warfare, and a great deal of international diplomacy, is facilitated by the practice of spying, and this practice is hardly possible without a fair degree of lying, though I suspect that much more is practised than is necessary or justified.

The requirements of discretion and of confidentiality can also create circumstances in which lying can seem justifiable. The casuists mentioned earlier were greatly exercised about problems arising from the confidentiality of the confessional, and much of what they say is relevant to contemporary professional codes of confidentiality This must have been important in the context of the Inquisition where confessors could have been asked whether their penitents had confessed to heretical acts or views. Some of the casuists held that it was permissible for a confessor to answer such questions with 'I don't know', thereby meaning that he didn't know in a way that could be publicly admitted. This 'mental reservation' as it was called, was allowed only because it would be generally known to any likely audience that knowledge gained in the confessional should not be revealed. Here, the mental reservation story is close to the reliance upon convention discussed earlier in the case of polite phrases. On the other hand, it is hard to see what the point of such a convention could be. Allowing a convention whereby people can say they are pleased to see a newcomer even when they are not has some point in avoiding unnecessary social unpleasantness and maintaining a norm of minimal politeness during social encounters. But the priestly falsehood seems to serve no point that would not be equally served by the open acknowledgement of what both audience and speaker already know, namely 'I can't reveal what I'm told in the confessional'. If the speaker is only absolved of telling a lie because he understands that his utterance will be taken in the non-standard sense that he somehow intends (as one might intend to conform to a greeting convention) then why not simply state the truth that the utterance is conventionally coded to mean?

The casuists also recognized equivocation as permissible in certain contexts, and, here, their position has some initial plausibility, though it was occasionally taken to absurd extremes. Equivocation involves taking advantage of an ambiguity in the question asked in order, for example, to avoid revealing a confidence. So one might tell pursuers of the innocent fugitive that he has gone to the bank, thereby sending them scurrying in futility to a nearby financial institution when the fugitive is actually by the river. This device faces the problem, noted by Bernard Williams, that it may not avoid the burden of lying anyway.[10] The issue here turns on the identity conditions for stating or saying. The equivocal utterance has two meanings and hence the speaker may be making one of two statements in the context. If we determine which one by the speaker's communicative intention then it is hard to avoid the conclusion that the speaker intends the audience to believe that the fugitive has gone to the nearby financial institution.[11] But then surely the speaker has lied by issuing that statement intending the audience to thereby gain this false belief from the speaker's words and embodied overt intention. It is irrelevant whether there is some other interpretation of the utterance that makes it true since that is not the meaning that the speaker intends the audience to take.

In any case, many find the use of such ingenuity (even when strongly restricted to special circumstances, as it was by the major casuists) morally dubious, if not repugnant, and think it better to lie boldly in the exceptional cases. They may be right. Certainly, the outright lie will often afford the fugitive better protection, though the casuistic options

---

[10] See Bernard Williams, *Truth and Truthfulness: An Essay in Genealogy* (Princeton: Princeton University Press, 2002), 103. Williams also considers the somewhat unlikely interpretation that the equivocator made no assertion at all, but merely pretended to assert. He points out that this has the unwelcome outcome that there is no need for the proposition that the hearer is invited to believe to be true. This follows because the equivocator avoids lying by not asserting at all, not by somehow asserting something true.

[11] On H. P. Grice's analysis, the matter is more complex, but the point remains essentially the same. See Grice, 'Utterer's Meaning and Intentions', *Philosophical Review*, 78 (Apr. 1969), 147–77; and for Grice's final words on these matters, see *Studies in the Way of Words* (Cambridge, Mass.: Harvard University Press, 1989).

are intended to preserve more effectively the agent's habits of speaking truthfully. It is a moot point whether the development of what the critics would see as the skills of deviousness is too great a cost to pay for risking habits of direct mendacity, especially where the risk is in reality slight. Moreover, either disposition treats the audience in a manipulative fashion that at least requires a very good reason to justify it.

In fact, the deviousness that worries the critics points to a particular problem in contemporary politics. The examples mentioned at the end of the section above on definition, including President Bush's State of the Union claim about what the British government had 'learned' about Iraq's effort to get uranium from Africa, are important because the traditional emphasis on the wrong of lying can make it seem as if other forms of deception are morally unimportant or at least of lesser significance. The casuistic insistence upon the legitimacy, in some rare circumstances, of misleading without lying, even if it were accepted, can easily suggest that such misleading may generally be treated lightly. But misleading statements, evasions, omissions of important information, failures to correct false impressions, or selective truth-telling can in context be just as bad if not worse than outright lying. This is particularly so on those occasions in politics (common enough) when the public have a right to complete disclosure, frank information, or unvarnished truth. The popular vogue for 'transparent' government is a response by citizens to the fact that so many political communications are misleading, economical with the truth, or tangential to the central issues, even when they do not involve direct lies. Certainly discretion, confidentiality, and other legitimate grounds for occasional secrecy make an appeal to total transparency ridiculous, but the attraction of the slogan 'transparent government' lies in the widespread sense that politicians all too often massage, 'spin', and manipulate the truth beyond all reason and moral seriousness.

Nonetheless, as we have seen, the rejection of lying in all circumstances is hard to defend, which makes its defence by such intellectual giants as Augustine, Aquinas, and Kant something of a mystery. Not too great a mystery of course because the conclusions of great minds sometimes defy common sense, and their views sometimes embody what their equally eminent successors reject as mere mistakes. A principle of charity towards great thinkers is unacceptable if it fails to allow for such possibilities. Nonetheless, it is worth seeing whether there is an interpretation of the rigorist position that makes more sense of it, and even makes it come out true. Christine Korsgaard has attempted a rescue of Kant in this spirit, and without arguing the plausibility of her account as exegesis or extension of Kant's various texts, we should consider whether her rescue attempt offers a story that could make acceptable sense of a rigorist position on lying, whether it fits Kant's actual words or not.[12]

Korsgaard rejects a total prohibition on lying in the world as it is, but, drawing on John Rawls's categories of 'ideal theory' and 'non-ideal theory', she argues that such a prohibition makes sense as part of ideal theory. What this amounts to is the idea that in a world of ideally rational agents in which full compliance with the dictates of reason is assured, a complete prohibition on lying would be mandatory. In a world in which irrational and evil acts are common, however, lying may be morally permissible, even required, to deal with wrongdoing. Although the structures of ideal theory are somewhat different from the role of moral ideals in the actual world, there is some echo here of our earlier discussion of ideals. As seen in Chapter 3 I am sympathetic to a significant role for ideals in moral thinking, but the ideal/non-ideal theorizing provides a philosophical methodology for moral thinking (or some forms of moral thinking) that goes beyond my sympathies in a number of ways. In particular, it is unclear to me what conclusions we can draw for the real, messy world from the idealizations claimed to be appropriate to a world of perfect or even near-perfect compliance. There are many complexities to be considered regarding Rawls's actual use of the distinction, in particular its apparent restriction to issues of the justice of basic structures, so that Korsgaard's application of it to the matter of lying may go beyond the spirit of Rawls's usage in any case, but my basic worry concerns the sort of prioritizing of the ideal theory that seems to be involved as well as the problems involved in fitting it to non-ideal theory and circumstances.[13] Nonetheless, if we take some hint from Korsgaard's idea and think of truthfulness not as a categorical obligation for all circumstances, but as an ideal, we might see the total prohibition on lying as presenting the virtues of such an ideal so that lying or indeed other forms of verbal deception are to be strictly avoided unless circumstances, most notably those that involve conflict with another moral ideal, make for their justification.

---

[12] Christine M. Korsgaard, 'The Right to Lie: Kant on Dealing with Evil', *Philosophy and Public Affairs*, 15/4 (1986), 325–49.

[13] For a discussion of some problems with the Rawlsian use of the contrast between ideal and non-ideal theory see Liam Murphy, 'Institutions and the Demands of Justice', *Philosophy and Public Affairs*, 27/4 (1999), 251–91. Also his book, *Moral Demand in Non-Ideal Theory* (New York: Oxford University Press, 2000).

This approach may show something positive that underpins the intransigent objections to lying of some of the great philosophers, and it helps emphasize the fact that a great deal of the time lying itself remains a serious wrong.[14] An ideal of truthfulness might at least inherit some of the sternness of spirit in the Augustinian/Kantian rejection of lying without requiring a total ban on it in the real world. Hence if we allow exceptions to the prohibition on lying, we must guard against their spreading, and we should be particularly wary of establishing casual practices of deception lest we damage the ideal and erode the habit of truthfulness, and deceive ourselves about the necessity and value of lying. Confronted with the prospect of lying in a good cause it is a useful test (as Sissela Bok has suggested) to put yourself in the shoes of the victims and ask whether the lie (or for that matter, the indirect deception) would be acceptable to them when they know the full circumstances.[15] This won't work, of course, where the victims are such as the Nazi pursuers; it is intended more for the cases where the justification for lying invokes the good of those deceived, as when it is proposed that one should lie to the terminally ill patient about her condition, or where it invokes some more general and genuine good for others. A parallel consideration is to envisage whether, after the event, you could publicly defend (in a television interview for instance) the reasoning behind the exception you propose to make. This test is particularly relevant to the deceptions said to be necessary for public life.

LIES, DIRTY HANDS, AND DEMOCRACY

As we saw in earlier chapters, some claim, following Machiavelli, that politics is so different from other areas of life that normal moral virtues do not apply to it. This might appear a comforting doctrine for politicians (though alarming for the rest of us) but the fact is that politicians themselves seldom endorse it overtly, unless they are

[14] There are of course other elements in the rigorism of Augustine, Kant, and Aquinas. Both Kant and Aquinas, for instance, seem at times fixated on the idea that there is something special about the teleology of speech or communication that supports a total ban on lying. For an excellent discussion of this sort of thinking see Bernard Williams, *Truth and Truthfulness*, esp. 105–7.

[15] Sissela Bok, *Lying: Moral Choice in Public and Private Life* (New York: Vintage Books, 1989), 90–4. My earlier example of the surprise party would probably pass this test.

stuck for justifications. This returns us to the discussion of dirty hands and supreme emergency, and it is worth noticing the ways in which the case of lying differs from that of killing the innocent or torture. For most, perhaps all, of the permissible lying examined so far, one distinctive feature of dirty hands does not apply. This is the feature that what we find it 'necessary' to do nonetheless remains somehow morally wrong. Admittedly, there was reason to be puzzled by this feature, but it can seem plausible for some examples, such as that of the prisoner doctor Olga Lengyel where the agent of 'the necessary act' legitimately experiences moral distress and remorse. But the trivial lying of many jokes, the polite expressions of insincere pleasure, or the lie that guarantees the success of the surprise birthday party are such that there is surely something absurd in the suggestion that the deceiving remains in any way morally wrong. It would be even stranger, and perhaps morally obtuse, to claim that the person who lies to the Nazi thugs to save a refugee from persecution has done *anything* wrong, even permissibly. This is one reason why the rigorist view of lying typified by Augustine and Kant remains so implausible. Nor will it do to locate some residual wrong in the fact that lying is usually wrong, or in the terminology of W. D. Ross violates a 'prima facie' duty. The fact that lying is often, usually, normally or 'prima facie' wrong does not mean that in this specific case (say, lying to the Nazi) there is *any* moral taint in the action or upon the agent's character or any room for real regret.

Some cases may however be nearer to satisfying the dirty hands feature in question. The spy who not only lies to the enemy, but also has to deceive loved ones and close friends (often with lies) about the nature of his activities, may better fit the dirty hands description. Of course, this raises questions about the moral status of different forms of spying, questions which are beyond the scope of this inquiry. Sufficient to note that by considering this example I do not mean to suggest any unequivocal endorsement of the necessity of 'dirty tricks' and the full panoply of dubious activities mostly hidden from public view or scrutiny that go under the curious and expansive heading of 'intelligence'.

In the case of much political lying and other culpable deceptions, what is true is that democratic politics puts such a glare of publicity upon politicians, and such a premium upon their vote-getting capacities that they are under very strong temptation to lie or mislead their way out of trouble, into advantageous positions, and into gaining or maintaining power. Indeed, the pursuit of power in modern democracies is so bound up with processes of befuddling, deceiving, and conning the electorate that various forms of dishonesty, including bare-faced lying, have almost become a standard coinage. The more disreputable techniques of advertising and public relations have been influential in creating the phenomenon of 'spin' whereby the truth is effectively concealed from the public and a comforting ersatz-reality is given credence. Perhaps the most egregious example of this is the career of the astonishing Silvio Berlusconi in Italy whose utilisation of misinformation and 'the big lie' promulgated by his media monopolies is only an extreme version of tendencies at work elsewhere in democratic polities.[16] Rather than seek excuses for political deceit, we would do better to seek changes to the institutions of democratic politics so that there is not only less pressure to lie but greater protection for and access to the unvarnished truth.

Of course whatever reforms are made, temptations abound. But a temptation is not a justification or an excuse. An alarming aspect of so much democratic politics is the way in which politicians have come to treat their own plans or ambitions as justifying a distressing degree of lying and deception, as if the survival of this or that politician, policy, or party is tantamount to the aversion of massive disaster. And this is not restricted to the politicians, for the success of their spin is often dependent on compliant mass media, which, for various reasons, accept and often promote the ersatz reality. The media's role here is certainly complex, partly because the term 'media' covers such widely differing outlets, ranging from the BBC to scandal sheets and Fox News, not to mention 'bloggers'. Some are more compliant and manipulable than others, and sometimes the less compliant can compound the problem by exaggerating the significance of slips, evasions, errors, and confusions. An excessively adversarial relation between the media and politicians can create conditions in which politicians can view truthfulness as a liability because it will invariably be treated as weakness, disloyalty, or folly. Nonetheless, real as this problem is, the tendency of much of the media to compliance with incumbent political authority or favoured opposition groups, and to susceptibility to spin, is an even greater problem. The moral basis of democracy requires, amongst other things, that citizens are given genuine information about policies, about the capacity and honesty (or lack of it) of their actual and potential leaders, and about the reasons for policies and decisions. Various schemes have been proposed

---

[16] For a fascinating account of Berlusconi's political career see Alexander Stille, *The Sack of Rome: How a Beautiful European Country with a Fabled History and a Storied Culture Was Taken Over by a Man Named Silvio Berlusconi* (New York: Penguin, 2006).

for overcoming the problems posed by spin and media distortion but where so many of the wells of communication are poisoned, the task of implementing reform is very difficult. Casual and frequent resort to spin has eroded public trust in political leadership and is one of the principal reasons why our politicians are held in widespread contempt, and why many electorates are so cynical about democratic processes. A capacity to compromise and negotiate is essential to political life, but when everything, including character, is up for negotiation then the craft of politics becomes merely crafty and contempt is the proper response to it. This is the sad contempt encapsulated in Huck Finn's weary remark about politics to the slave Jim: 'All kings is mostly rapscallions.'

Index